Ned Fritz

Jim Alford

12/6/86

Realms of Beauty

The Wilderness Areas of East Texas

Realms of Beauty

The Wilderness Areas of East Texas

by Edward C. Fritz
Photographs by Jess Alford

University of Texas Press, Austin

First Edition, 1986

Requests for permission to reproduce material from this work
should be sent to Permissions, University of Texas Press,
Box 7819, Austin, Texas 78713-7819.

Library of Congress Cataloging-in-Publication Data

Fritz, Edward C., 1916–
    Realms of beauty.

    Includes index.
    1. Wilderness areas—Texas.   2. Natural history—
Texas.   I. Alford, Jess, 1933–   . II. Title.
QH105.T4F74   1986   508.764   86-11301
ISBN 0-292-76440-5
ISBN 0-292-76504-5 (pbk.)

Contents

Buttonbush Pond, Little Lake Creek Wilderness. *At the edge of the bottoms, an abandoned channel has dissipated into twin ponds lined with butterfly-attracting buttonbushes and fished by green-backed herons. This pond is tea colored with tannin from the leaves and roots of a thousand oaks.*

Prologue

Join me in an ode—an ode not to an urn, nor a nightingale, nor any other object or species, but to natural communities of myriad species. In particular, I praise the plant associations that comprise the natural heart of East Texas.

To give even broader import to the classic poetry, no species is an island, entire of itself. All species live in association with others. Given time, certain plants tend to grow near each other in environments favorable to the combination. Ecologists name these communities after the two or three most obvious species. For example, during the ice ages, American beech and southern magnolia became the dominant components of what is now known as beech/magnolia forest.

When men clearcut an ancient grove of beech and magnolia, and scrape or plow the soil, they eliminate from that place not merely beeches and magnolias but also beech-drops, a brown flower that grows from the roots of the beech trees; crane-fly orchids, which depend on chemicals in fallen beech leaves; and some twenty molds, bacteria, and animals, including at least six species of butterflies and moths that feed almost exclusively on beech foliage or lay eggs in beech mulch.

The beech, in turn, benefits from liverworts, algae, bacteria, and insects that produce the proper soil; fungi that assist the seeds in germination; dogwoods and other calcium-pumping trees to replenish vital minerals used up by beeches; and moths and butterflies that pollinate the tree blossoms to facilitate fertilization, along with a host of other bacteria, insects, and birds that control the moths, butterflies, and other creatures that eat various parts of the tree. The beech also needs microscopic species that feed on the bacteria that plague beech trees. To compete best with other species in the South, beeches associate with well-spaced southern magnolias, which block out almost every ray of sunlight under their crowns. In a cleared area, beech seedlings also depend upon pioneer trees like sweet gums, which shade out other plants so that shade-loving beech trees can compete.

If we complete the current process of eliminating all the ancient beech/magnolia groves (mainly to grow pines), we shall lose forever the complex interrelationships and many of the species in this plant community. Even if we save some beeches and magnolias together in gardens, parks, and arboretums, we shall never be able to reconstruct a beech/magnolia community in full.

We could tell a similar story about the longleaf pine/scrub oak upland parkland community and other habitats that are disappearing under modern coniferization practices and human development in general. This book is an ode to the evanescent beauty of such natural life systems.

But beauty is only brain deep. Old-growth and intermediate communities have other values, as well. They serve as living museums to educate present and future generations on the natural heritage of the region. They provide authentic laboratories where scientists may engage in research on such vital subjects as survival and evolution. And they constitute gene pools for substances and products useful to humankind.

When human beings remove examples of a species, like the natural ancestor of corn, from their natural ecosystem and raise them through many generations, the species becomes more susceptible to diseases and other natural hazards. Horticulturalists and others are continuously strengthening our domesticated varieties by transfusing into them the genes of natural ancestors or other related species, still in the wild. Natural species are more resistant because of continued interrelationships and competition with all kinds of plants, animals, viruses, bacteria, fungi, and other forms of life.

Some wild species can adapt to civilization. The cardinal and mockingbird fare well in suburban environments. But

many species cannot. Even if we were able in managed forests to raise an endangered species like the red-cockaded
woodpecker, the survivors would probably weaken genetically, because of the decline in natural selection. Therefore,
to save many species, we must save their natural habitats.

We do not yet know all the species that human beings
will be needing. Researchers and enterprising business folk
continue annually to discover uses of additional plants, animals, fungi, and bacteria for medicines, foods, fibers, dyes,
manufacturing catalysts, and other products.

But even if we knew what species we will need, we could
not guarantee our future supply by saving their seeds in
seed banks or their living specimens in greenhouses. Ecologists are continuously discovering incredible interdependen-
cies, like those among the bee, orchid, and mycelia (dis-
cussed under the rose pogonia and grass-pink orchid photographs, pp. 65, 68). When we remove any species from its
habitat or disrupt any of its neighbors, whether above or below the soil or stream bottom, we may be dooming that species to extinction, at least in the area we disrupt.

So we see that we need to preserve examples of as many
biotic communities as possible. Many readers may be im-
pressed more by utilitarian values (as in survival of the human species) than by sheer beauty (as in Keats' Grecian
urn). Once they realize that plant communities are essential
to human progress, these readers will appreciate our wildernesses more deeply than before.

From yet another view, the freer a forest is from the ma-
nipulations of human beings, the more clearly the spirit of
earth and sky is manifested in the marvelous processes that
we sense.

Let our eyes and minds now drink the beauty and sing the
praises of six areas where, by the grace of humankind, East
Texas plant communities may survive and evolve as long as
life endures in this verdant region.

Acknowledgments

A lot of people have contributed positively or strangely to
this opus. My mother made me an outdoorsman by driving
me out of the house with the noise of her vacuum cleaner.
My father took all of us boys in the neighborhood fishing
along wild streams. Miss Castelaz taught me grammar at
Pershing School. Miss Stillwell introduced me to John
Keats' poetry at Tulsa Central High School. Dr. Eula White-
house started me on Texas wild flowers. Alexander Sprunt,
Jr., hooked me onto ecosystems at a National Audubon Society summer camp near Kerrville.

By clearcutting all available commercial timber in national forests, the U.S. Forest Service inspired me to work
for preservation of wildernesses.

In 1977, I asked Billy Hallmon to find some wildernesses
and he found Graham Creek bottoms and Indian Mounds.
Autra and Mary Fant revealed to me Beech Bottom. John
Walker showed me the treasures of Big Slough. Raymond
Edgar, James Jackson, Larry Shelton, and George Russell,
those of the sharp eyes of eagles, discovered many champion
trees and Forest Service atrocities.

Four congressmen were essential: John Bryant sponsored
the East Texas Wilderness Bill, which saved five areas from
the Forest Service long enough to write a book about them.
Steve Bartlett talked the Republicans into letting it pass.
Martin Frost gave us the third co-sponsor that John Seiber-
ling, of Ohio, required before he would work the bill
through Interior Committee. Lloyd Bentsen and John Tower
got the bill through the Senate. Charles Wilson added the
concepts that made Upland Island and Indian Mounds large
enough to be viable.

The four of these congressmen who have visited our wildernesses have been honored by having big trees named for them:

> The John Bryant State Champion Shagbark Hickory near Graham Creek in Upland Island.

> The Charlie Wilson State Champion Loblolly Pine near the Neches River in Big Slough.

> The Steve Bartlett National Champion Longleaf Pine in Upland Island.

> The John Seiberling State Champion Cherrybark Oak in Upland Island.

Dr. Jack McCullough organized the scientific study that verified the values of Upland Island. Drs. Elray Nixon and Bill Mahler checked out Beech Bottom and other areas. Bob Slaughter provided me with more geological information than I could grasp.

David Wilson drew the maps for Big Slough, Turkey Hill, Indian Mounds, and Little Lake Creek and figure 1. Billy Hallmon drew the map for Upland Island and figure 2.

Genie Fritz shared the entire experience, including reading my handwriting and typing several drafts of this before the editors and I were satisfied. Ann Smith filled a rush re-typing role.

Many a time, Jess Alford went charging down to East Texas from Dallas to photograph a scene at just the right time. James Jackson, the generous, contributed key photographs.

For these and everyone else who helped, I invoke the strength of oaks and the fragrance of magnolias.

And I express my deepest gratitude to Earth for the diversity that she has brought forth, for the examples of her greatness that she has ruggedly retained, and for the privilege that I enjoy to share those blessings with you.

Realms of Beauty

The Wilderness Areas of East Texas

The Deep and Varied Forests and the Splendid Samples That Survive

Introduction

Some ten thousand or more years ago, when the first humans ventured into what is now known as Deep East Texas, they found a satisfying place to live, rich in foods, fibers, and scenes. The fertile soils were sandy loam, drained by a network of streams. The highest hills were more than four hundred feet while the lowest river bottom was less than one hundred feet above sea level. A verdant cloak of plant life graced the entire area.

Today the topography remains essentially the same. The plant life has changed drastically.

During the occupation of East Texas by the hunter-gatherers, the great ice sheet to the north receded, causing a change of climate and an attendant shift in vegetation and wildlife.

But the climate has not changed much since a thousand years ago. We know from their relics that the Caddo, who by that time had settled in villages near the Neches and Sabine rivers, hunted the same species of animals and gathered the same species of plants as explorers De Soto and La Salle observed there in 1542 and 1586.

These Europeans found a magnificent diversified forest, varying with the terrain—in the bottomlands, towering oaks, hickories, and sweet gums; in the sloughs, giant bald cypresses and tupelo gums; along the slopes, American beech and southern magnolia, with white oak and loblolly pine; and on the uplands, southern red oak and shortleaf pine, with parklands of tall longleaf pines and smaller bluejack oaks dominating the deepest sands.

Many other vegetation associations lent diversity to this pattern, including occasional seeps where carnivorous plants abounded. And in early spring, the carpet of the slopes dappled forth with an ephemeral display of spring cress and orchids—coralroot, southern twayblade, and vernal ladies' tresses—which disappeared, blade and flower, when the trees leafed out.

Wildlife was abundant in this great forest, from squirrels to black bears, and from hooded warblers to red-shouldered hawks.

The Caddo knew these forests well and utilized hundreds of species of indigenous plants, most of which modern foresters disdain. For example, consider the oaks and hickories. Their acorns and nuts were among the staples of the Caddo. They ate them raw. They toasted them. They cooked them with other foods. They used the limbs for firewood. They revered oak and hickory trees because deer and squirrels, important sources of food and fiber, browsed on the twigs all year and fattened on the nuts to survive the winter cold.

Today, Texas foresters look upon most oaks and hickories as weeds that deprive the commercial pines of water and nutrients. Foresters girdle or poison the big hardwoods, burn the saplings to prevent them from maturing, and, after clearcutting the survivors, push them into windrows to make room for pines. Only hunters and noncommercial woods wanderers still appreciate the oaks and hickories for their fruits, their benefits to wildlife, and their beauty and majesty.

Unlike the terrain, the vegetation has changed in the past one hundred years. Around the turn of the century, loggers removed the southern magnolias, black cherries, and white ash for furniture, boxes, bats, and even railroad ties. Timber companies harvested the larger trees. The forests grew back, but cattle raisers cleared for pasture, oil companies and governments built roads, settlements became towns, and towns grew into cities. Hunters exterminated the black bear from these areas, probably forever.

Around the 1950s came the crowning blow, indiscriminate clearcutting, in which the foresters followed each harvest of larger trees by bulldozing all remaining vegetation and "regenerating" with one or the other species of pine, generally loblolly. By this practice, "foresters" plan to convert the entire forest into tree farms. The only exceptions are tiny stringers of "den trees" and, in national forests, some small recreation areas.

Fortunately, in 1984, the East Texas Wilderness Act, sponsored by Congressman John Bryant and Senator Lloyd Bentsen, saved from the bulldozer five sizable wildernesses. Congressmen Steve Bartlett and Martin Frost and Senator John Tower co-sponsored the bill. The Forest Service has temporarily deferred from cutting an additional sample of our East Texas natural heritage. As shown on the map, the five areas form an angular pattern across East Texas, like the horn of Taurus, with its point in Sabine County and its bases in Montgomery and Houston counties. Although the five wildernesses have been logged in places, each contains some stands that retain the diversity of deep forests as they were when the Caddoan groups roved there. And the logged stands will restore themselves, given the time.

Thus, in places, we are still privileged to see long-ago scenes, like creek banks where the vanishing yellow lady's slipper orchid continues to bloom and shaded swales where the rare Swainson's warbler has nested every year for more than a thousand years.

You have to take a quantum leap backward to understand why these five wildernesses differ from each other. Although close together in space, they are eons apart (see fig. 1). Their surfaces date back to contrasting eras. Therefore, their soils sustain some different plant communities.

One more thought—the six areas coming into view are not in the Big Thicket. That richly vegetated region lies farther southeast, toward Beaumont, where it is represented by the Big Thicket National Preserve. The Big Thicket rainfall is ten to twenty inches heavier per year than in the wildernesses. Its average temperature is warmer, its soil is younger, and, therefore, as would be expected, its vegetation and scenery differ from that of the six areas we shall here portray.

As we take a look at these ancient plant communities, we turn first to the wilderness that is located on the oldest geological formation, situated farthest from the coast, and thence, in order, to the wilderness on the youngest formation, closest to the coast. Finally, we gaze upon Beech Bottom, an old world in itself.

Figure 1. *In simple form, this illustration reflects the ages of selected geological formations that presently appear at the surface of the five East Texas wildernesses, and, for comparison, Big Thicket National Preserve. Each formation was originally laid down under an ancient sea, swamp, or river and was buried and compacted under later formations. The rising of the Rocky Mountains tilted all formations upward about 1 percent. As the Gulf receded and advanced, eons of rains and streams wore off the layers from the top down, exposing the present surfaces in broad bands, like plywood sawed at one end on a broad bias.*

Because of this tilt, the farther north a wilderness is from the Gulf, the older is the formation that is exposed there. Since our five wildernesses occupy different formations by a span of 30 million years, they exemplify substantial differences in soils. These, in turn, produce different plant associations.

Big Slough contains an example of the oldest outcrop among our five wildernesses. Some 50 million years ago, long after the dinosaurs trundled here, this area was tens of fathoms beneath an Eocene sea. The sand bottom gradually became the sandstone formation that we now call the Sparta. As the land emerged, birds and small mammals, the size of kittens, prevailed here.

After a few million years, under a later Eocene sea, the Cook Mountain layer was formed. As that sea receded from the surface of what is now Turkey Hill, the first carnivores, squirrel sized, hunted across the mud flats and river deltas. Gradually, some mammals developed to twice the size of a rhinoceros. Some mammals returned to the water as whales. More seas advanced. More formations followed, including the Yegua, which now resurfaces in a band encompassing Indian Mounds Wilderness. The clays and rocks of two subsequent formations, the Whitsett and the Catahoula, from 42 million down to 25 million years old, can be seen in parts of Upland Island Wilderness. During the Catahoula, in the Oligocene series, tropical climes prevailed. Palms became the dominant plants, but pines began to spread. Most of the mammals were the size of cats and dogs. (Dr. Ernest Ledger, geologist at Stephen F. Austin State University, writes that the petrified wood in the Catahoula rock outcrop on the southern end of Upland Island "provides the only record of Oligocene forest and climates known in Texas.")

Later came the Fleming formation, in the Miocene series. The Fleming surfaces along a band that includes Little Lake Creek Wilderness, southernmost of the five wildernesses. In

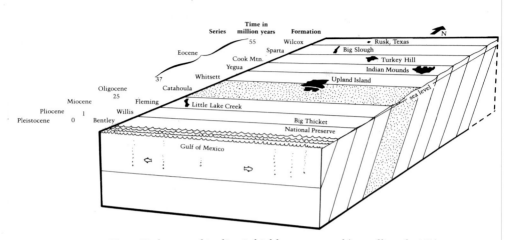

Note: Underground incline is highly exaggerated (actually only 1%); thickness of formations not drawn to scale.

the millions of years when the Fleming was laid down, there were periods when the land above sea level, all the way to the Rockies, was covered with well-spaced pines in a parkland of grasses, grazed by many horselike species, large and small.

The northern edge of the Big Thicket National Preserve includes outcrops of the Fleming formation and major subsequent formations, laid down as deltas formed and hardened during the Pliocene series.

Broadleaf trees joined the pines, at times covering the continental United States and Canada. Twelve million years ago many ponds formed.

About 10 million years ago, prairies prevailed in East Texas. In the last 2 million years, during each Ice Age, the northern forests would retreat to East Texas, far south of the ice, and then follow the ice back northward, leaving here such northern species as American beech and mockernut hickory to mingle with the southern magnolia, Louisiana palmetto, and longleaf pine. This mingling continued through the advent of humans from Asia more than ten thousand years ago. In our East Texas wildernesses, this rich mixture of northern and southern species persists to this very day.

Each wilderness chapter includes a map of the wilderness, as well as directions for getting there and where to walk when you are there. As *Realms of Beauty* goes to press, chances appear good that Congress will authorize additions to all five wildernesses. In April 1986, Congressman Charles Wilson, of Lufkin, introduced a bill to that effect. The additions would mainly even out the boundaries and add key natural areas, like previously omitted stretches of Turkey Creek in Turkey Hill Wilderness.

The additions are indicated on the maps by letters and striped areas. They are already open to the public except for the following private tracts: *B* in Big Slough, *A* in Turkey Hill, and *A* and *B* in Upland Island. If you approach those four tracts from inside the wilderness, look for the small yellow Forest Service boundary markers or small white wilderness markers. If neither type of marker is any longer

there, this will mean that the Forest Service will have ac-
quired the addition and you may enter.

What to Take In and Out

1. Water. Take enough drinking water for your entire stay.
   Some of us drink from the springs and branches without
   regret, but not where cattle have reached the water. At
   least, you can safely wash dishes in the springs, branches,
   and creeks, and bathe where the water is deep enough.
2. Food. Carry enough in, and also munch on the blue-
   berries of four species, spring through fall.
3. Waste. Carry out all containers, wrappers, and remnants
   of food and other products. Bury other waste.
4. Clothing. Wear hiking or walking shoes and jeans or
   other tough slacks in case you encounter briers. Carry a
   complete change of clothing in your car, in case you encounter wet weather or soggy creek bottoms. In hot, dry
   weather many people wear shorts. The average annual
   rainfall ranges from 45 to 50 inches, scattered throughout the year but lighter in summer and fall when showers
   are usually short.
5. Camping equipment. Any tent will do, the lighter the
   better. You can camp within a few feet of all parking
   places mentioned in the text, or you can backpack in for
   two or three miles to our suggested primitive campsites,
   or you can stay wherever you choose.
6. Pests. Carry repellents.
7. Take-outs. Don't take anything out, except junk left by
   others. Don't collect plants and animals unless you have
   a scientific permit.

Precautions

1. Snakes. Cottonmouth moccasins lie near water. Copper-
   heads hide in several habitats. There may be coral snakes
   and timber rattlesnakes, although we know of no recent
   records. These poisonous species feed primarily at night

and do not aggress toward humans, but watch your step, especially at night, so that you do not tread on one. The other snakes are nonpoisonous. All are beneficial.

2. Insects. Mosquitoes operate spring through fall, everywhere except the highest uplands. For most people, a mosquito bite itches only for a few minutes. Chiggers are mainly in disturbed locations, such as along roadsides and in clearcuts. Occasionally, horseflies attack people at certain hours, but they can be swatted by hand. Where the sun reaches the ground, there may be a fire ant mound, 2 to 24 inches high, covered with grainy sand particles. Don't stand within two feet of one.

   Some of us handle all insects by wearing slacks and long-sleeved shirts and avoiding roadsides, clearcuts, and fire ant mounds. Others apply "Off," "Cutter's," etcetera, when needed.

3. Noxious plants. Poison-oak and poison ivy grow on ground and trees in some spots. Avoid all low plants and vines with sets of three leaves. Poison sumac grows in seeps, baygalls, and other wet places. It has compound leaves, comprised of seven to thirteen leaflets with reddish petioles. Don't touch it. If you happen to touch any of these, wash the affected skin within thirty minutes.

4. Deer season. In deer season, wear an orange hat and jacket. Opening weekend is the worst. After that, you will encounter few hunters except during the first hour after dawn and the last hour before dark. Deer season usually begins in mid-November and lasts for two months. As an additional precaution in deer season, talk or sing as you walk through dense vegetation.

5. Finding your way. Take a compass. Federal boundaries are marked by small yellow plates, facing outward at occasional intervals. Respect private property. Stay on federal land. If you have time in advance, order a Forest Service map, Class A, for each National Forest involved, from U.S. Forest Service, P.O. Box 969, Lufkin, Texas 75901.

Big Slough

It seems strange that the smallest wilderness, the one that lies farthest from the Gulf of Mexico and draws the least rainfall, holds the most water on its surface.

Big Slough covers only 3,040 acres, some of which have never been logged and none since 1968. The edge of this wilderness is fifteen miles from Alto on U.S. 69. Of the five national forest wildernesses, it lies closest to Dallas and the dry West. Yet, other than its arid southern upland, this wilderness is the wettest and therefore contains natural areas that are strikingly different from any others in Texas.

Shaped like a rabbit standing on its haunches with ears held down, the area is mostly within the one-hundred-year floodplain of the usually clear, clean, and serene Neches River, which comprises eleven of the twelve miles along the eastern boundary of the wilderness.

The other Texas wildernesses have their wet places, but Big Slough Wilderness is close to wetness from head to toe (except for a dry "heel"). Its northern half embraces a sluggish watercourse named Big Slough. Southwest of the slough spreads a large marsh maintained by beavers.

Along the slough, in a sinuous ribbon, thrives an association that most plant ecologists from other regions have never described—overcup oak/mayhaw/planer tree. The slough is in the middle. On both sides, with feet in the water, grow planer trees, a species of the southern wetlands. On the outer band of each ribbon are towering overcups, which compete best in terrain where water covers their roots at least three months of the year. Their cups virtually

Slough Habitat. *Spanish moss drapes a sweet gum tree above the slow side stream. A planer tree on the right rounds out this distinctive habitat of the Gulf Coastal Plain ecosystem. When the water is high like this, Big Slough and the Neches River form an unmatchable 8-mile canoe loop.*

Snag. *Fungi bracket a dead tree (snag). The shrub behind it, on the left, is a planer tree, also known as water elm. In this pond beavers and alligators flourish. Above, pileated woodpeckers cackle. In some hours, the only other sound is the crash of a falling limb.*

close over their acorns, slowing the rotting process in their wet abode so that some are left to sprout during a drier spell. Under these oaks are the mayhaws, whose fruits the Indians ate raw or cooked and the pioneers jarred as jelly.

The national champion planer tree also grows here. Ducks devour the fruit of this species all winter.

Big Slough, itself, is a partly abandoned channel of the Neches River, rich in channel catfish. Between the slough and the Neches lies a bottomland island containing five square miles of never-harvested southern river-bottom hardwood forest. On the east side of the island, the Upper Neches flows southward in a six-mile arc. On the west side, the slough completes the circle, joining the Neches at both ends of its arc. This circle provides a famous canoe trail.

River birch, black willow, sycamore, and elderberry line the Neches, backed up by large American elms, Shumard oaks, and swamp chestnut oaks. The broad lower leaves of the latter oak, with their wavy margins, reach a foot in length. In autumn, they fall in heaps. Sometimes you have to kick your way through them.

The rest of the island between the slough and the river is shaded by large cherrybark oaks, swamp chestnut oaks, bitternut hickories, cedar elms, and sugarberries, darkly shading a carpet of leaf litter. So little sunlight penetrates the canopy that greenbrier, rattan, and fox grape vines climb rapidly to the ceiling, leaving the ground open to easy walking.

After heavy rains, the river rises, spreads across the island, and sweeps between the tree trunks, curling in an eddy below every big tree. Weak canoeists should postpone their voyages for two or three days until the water recedes.

Southwest of the slough is a series of beaver and alligator ponds covering hundreds of acres. Buttonbushes surround the ponds, attracting millions of butterflies. White rose-mallows bloom in profusion. This species of wild hibiscus has blossoms six inches in diameter with rose-purple throats.

The wetness of this wilderness provides an advantage in addition to distinctiveness of habitat—Big Slough is too swampy for livestock. We have seen many deer tracks here, but no sign of cattle.

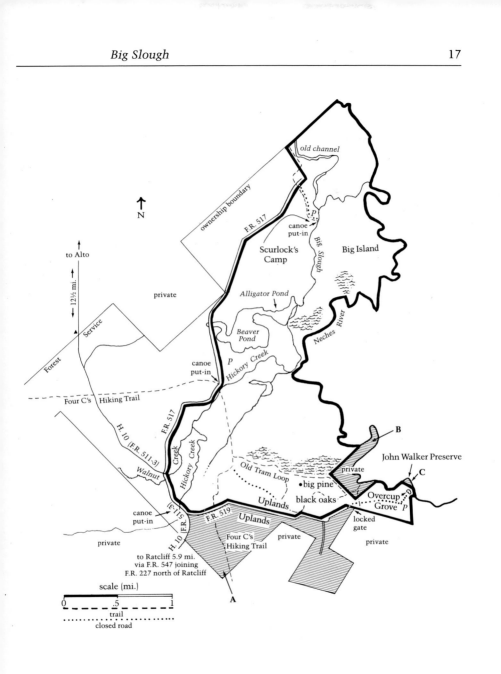

Mood of Beaver Pond. *Over-cup oaks stand in water several months a year. Their acorns are completely covered by their cups, enabling them to survive wetness better than other oaks. But if the "toes" of this species are in the water for too short a period each year, other oaks and gums will eventually move in and crowd them out.*

Crossing the Slough. *In rainy spells, the only dry way to get onto the big island is by canoe or by fallen log. But the wildness you reach is worth the effort, a solid canopy of oaks and gums over 100 feet high, never cut, never developed, seldom visited by humans. (Photo by James R. Jackson)*

Copperhead. *These snakes abound in the five East Texas wildernesses. They never strike humans unless molested, and seldom then. You can tell by its green tail that this one is young. One of the four species of poisonous snakes in East Texas, the copperhead is generally small here. Nevertheless, most hunters shoot every copperhead on sight, as an expression of fear and superiority. This snake eats mainly insects and small rodents.*

Big and Little Sisters. *The wilderness spawns a proliferation of mushrooms in all colors and sizes, up to 12 inches across. This one is an imperial mushroom (*Amanita caesarea*), related to the deadly poisonous Destroying Angel. The rootlike mycelia of this fungus extend for dozens of meters through the soil, decomposing the fallen debris into nitrogen and other nutrients needed by living plants. In turn, the mycelia fasten to pine roots and obtain beneficial products of the photosynthesis of the plants. Pines and certain other plants cannot live without fungi, and some fungi cannot live without those plants. Clearcutting interferes with this vital connection.*

Why does the northern half of this wilderness hold so
much water? The beaver dams help. More basically, in the
middle of the wilderness the land begins to rise southward
toward an ancient ridge, a hundred feet high, which, like a
dike, diverts the Neches eastward around it, leaving a large
hollow of ponds and silt north of the ridge.

Hickory Creek flows into this hollow from the west, di-
viding the northern body of the wilderness from the southern ridge. In rainy springtime, this creek serves as a second
canoe trail. Along the creek a different set of trees predomi-
nates—shagbark hickory, Carolina basswood, white oak,
and large loblolly pine. Shagbarks, with their loose plates up
to five feet long, and basswoods, with fruits appended to fly-
ing wings, are disappearing throughout the South.

At the east end of the ridge, a 100-acre "big toe" of
wilderness juts into the river. In this toe looms a stately
grove of tall overcup oaks and water hickories. Their dense
foliage muffles all but tiny shafts of sunlight, creating a ca-
thedral-like aspect reminiscent of redwood parks, though on
a smaller scale.

From the "big toenail," or Overcup Grove, the bottomland rises under big white oaks to primitive camping sites,
which overlook the grove and the river.

A line of oaks, hickories, and ironwoods extends westward from Overcup Grove along the northern base of the
high ridge. When you walk southward a short distance up
the ridge, you see an increase in pines and a shift in hardwood species. One of the loblolly pines is the largest in the
national forests in Texas, 14 feet in circumference at breast
height and 152 feet tall. Its huge bole is free of branches to a
height of 60 feet.

Nearby is the rare green rein orchis. Uphill is the rare
green adder's mouth orchid. Still farther uphill, some black
oaks survive near the southwestern extremity of their
range.

On the highest elevations, shortleaf pines tower over
southern red oaks, post oaks, and farkleberries. In spots
where the rains run off the fastest, sundew, red buckeye, and
narrow-leaf yucca thrive and Allegheny chinkapins, with
their delicious little chestnuts, are making a last stand. The
geological formation that outcrops here is the Sparta, oldest

of all in East Texas wildernesses. Thus, our smallest, oldest, and wettest wilderness, rich in overcups, planer trees, beavers, and canoe trails, also has elevations where we, its latest natural inhabitants, can survey this lush realm from vantage points on dry ground.

Access to Big Slough

You can reach the wilderness from the north (see below), but the usual route to Big Slough is from the south via the small town of Ratcliff, on Texas 103, 16 miles east of Crockett or 31 miles west of Lufkin. From Ratcliff, take paved Farm Road (F.M.) 227 north for 1 mile, then graveled Forest Road (F.R.) 547 northward for about 3 miles, then sandy F.R. 533 northeastward for about 7/10 mile, then sandy Houston County (H.) 10 northward for 1 2/10 miles to its intersection with F.R. 519 at the southwestern corner of the wilderness.

From that intersection you have two choices:

1. You can turn left and continue northwestwardly on H. 10 another mile, turn right on once-paved F.R. 517, and go northeastward for another mile to a crossing of the Four C's Hiking Trail.

A short distance north from this trail crossing, you can park and walk eastward 200 yards along an old jeep road to the bank of Hickory Creek, where grows a giant loblolly. Large hardwoods shade this walk, and many species of shrubs, grasses, and other herbs carpet the forest floor.

If you continue to drive northward on F.R. 517 for 2 more miles (3 miles from H. 10), you will come to the end of the old paving. From there, you can walk eastward along an abandoned sand road about 1/4 mile to Scurlock's Camp on Big Slough. This location no longer has any structures.

2. From the intersection of H. 10 and F.R. 519, at the southwestern corner of the wilderness, you can turn right and drive eastward along F.R. 519 for about 200 yards to the crossing of the Four C's Hiking Trail heading northward into the wilderness. If you walk this trail northward about 1/2 mile, you can turn east on the Old Tram Loop Trail. In almost a mile, at a wet place, if you head uphill (south) you may find the state champion loblolly pine. You can return

Four C's Hiking Trail. *This long trail enters and traverses the southwest quadrant, across the driest ground in our most-water-covered wilderness. The light green leaves on the left belong to an American beauty-berry shrub. The darker leaves below them are wax myrtle.*

The High and the Fallen. *Beneath 100-foot water oaks and willow oaks lies a down log, symbol of an old-growth forest. This is a typical scene along the west bank of the Neches near the northern tip of Big Slough Wilderness.*

to your car by the same route or cross-country. From there, you can continue eastward on F.R. 519 about 1½ miles to a locked gate, where you can park. Walk eastward on the road into the wilderness about ²⁄₁₀ mile farther, past where a private jeep road branches north to a 58-acre private tract on the river. Continue eastwardly another half-mile to Overcup Grove alongside the 3-acre John Walker Preserve, open to the public.

Access from the north is via Texas 21 out of Alto, which is also on U.S. 69. You drive southwest from Alto on Texas 21 for 8 miles to F.R. 511-3 (also known as H. 10); turn left and take it southeast 6 miles to the edge of the wilderness at F.R. 517. Or you can leave F.R. 511-3 only 1 mile southeast of Texas 21 and turn left on a 1-mile-long road to Neches Overlook and the north end of the Four C's Hiking Trail, whence you can backpack 9 miles to the wilderness.

Camping

Six miles south of the wilderness, 1 mile west of Ratcliff on Texas 103, the Forest Service operates Lake Ratcliff Recreation Area, containing seventy sites. A fee is charged. This facility includes water, restrooms, showers, lake fishing, swimming beach, bathhouse, and small concession stand.

Primitive camping is allowed anywhere in the wilderness. The best current spots, in ascending order of privacy, include Scurlock's Camp on Big Slough near the end of F.R. 517, Hickory Creek off F.R. 517 1²⁄₁₀ miles north of H. 10, the Uplands along the south boundary (250 feet in elevation), and the slope above Overcup Grove in the southeastern appendage of the wilderness.

There is also primitive camping at Neches Overlook at the northern end of the Four C's Hiking Trail, 9 miles from the wilderness. From here you can scan the Neches valley, including Caddo Mounds State Historic Preserve, 3 miles to the northeast (a place worth visiting).

The Forest Service does not recommend the streams and ponds for drinking, although there is no known pollution. Always pitch a tent, unless you don't mind risking a thunderstorm at 2:00 A.M. For locations of primitive camping spots, see "P's" on the map.

Four C's Hiking Trail

Although this 19-mile trail traverses the wilderness for only 2 miles, we recommend it as a way to get there on foot from south or north. It starts or ends at Lake Ratcliff Recreation Area. The north end is at Neches Overlook, a forty-foot bluff above the river, formerly an established campground and still good for primitive camping.

The trail is well marked. In the wilderness it is shaded by tall hardwoods and pines. Footbridges cross the larger streams.

The trail outside the wilderness crosses several roads, enabling groups to set up car shuttles for walks of different lengths. Outside the wilderness, the trail passes through several recent clearcuts, which the Forest Service has planted to pine.

Canoe Trails

Big Slough Canoe Trail is the only natural full-circuit stream trail in Texas. You can float 8 miles in a big loop, through beautiful forests well populated with birds, including prothonotary warblers and yellow-crowned night herons. There are no rapids. The put-in place closest to a road is Scurlock's Camp, 1/4 mile from the north end of F.R. 517. Travel clockwise, so as to go down the Neches River and up the smaller slough, which may become too low for floating in dry summers. During the annual spring floods, the southward current in the slough, as well as in the river (and sometimes all the way in between), is too strong for the average canoeist. Oaks, pines, and green ashes line the banks of the Neches for the next 130 miles—the longest remaining stretch of river in Texas listed as swimmable and fishable.

Shagbark Hickory/Nutmeg Hickory Bottomland. *The closer, rougher-barked granddaddy is a nutmeg hickory, known to only a few scattered floodplains in the South. The shagbark hickory, behind it, belongs to another vanishing species. When these species dominate a stand, very little vegetation grows beneath them. This rare scene is near Turkey Creek*

Nutmeg and Shagbark Hickories, Pawpaws and Indian Pinks

A Bountiful Visit to Turkey Hill

Inspired (although through a territorial imperative) by the full moon, a chuck-will's-widow sang loudly from eight to ten in the evening—"Chuck widdle's widow, chuck widdle's widow," a hundred times in a row, then a minute's pause, and then at it again, setting our mood for a bountiful visit to the depths of Turkey Hill Wilderness Area. When the nighthawk-like bird tuned off, the barred owl began hooting. At five in the morning, the chuck-will's-widow picked up again, alerting us to prepare for our exploration.

We were camping on Turkey Hill, only three-fourths of a mile west of Farm Road (F.M.) 705, which frames the east boundary of the wilderness. It was May 14, too late for the ephemeral orchids, too early for the big Carolina lilies, but we hoped to find fascinations of some kind.

In March, we had walked northward from this oak-clad hill a few hundred yards to Clear Branch and had followed it eastward, where we had exulted over the numbers of blossoming coralroot and southern twayblade orchids, spring cress, and the leaves of crane-fly orchids. But these components of our early ephemeral community had disappeared in April.

Again, as in March, we headed down the hill into the forest of widely spaced beeches, oaks, and loblolly pines and admired their stature. But this time, we selected a riffle, stepped over the tiny stream, and proceeded toward the northwest, along the beech slopes. The tree canopy shaded us the entire way and generally was so dense that the understory was well spaced, making it easy to walk while looking upward at the American redstarts, pine warblers, parula warblers, hooded warblers, and red-eyed, white-eyed, and yellow-throated vireos.

After a mile and a half of climbing low ridges and descending to intermittent streams, we followed a trickle down to the broad floodplain of Turkey Creek. That was a different world.

For a depth of about a quarter of a mile, the Turkey Creek bottoms nourished trees and flowers of almost every species known to the hardwood bottomlands of East Texas. The trees forming the under canopy were more than one hundred feet in height. Their trunks rose forty feet without a limb. One water oak was thirteen feet around.

Beneath these giants, three species gave the bottoms an exotic appearance: the pawpaw, green dragon, and Indian pink. With leaves up to a foot long and half as wide, pawpaws dominated our view of the understory near Turkey Creek. In Texas, the pawpaw is usually a mere shrub. But these pawpaws measured as large as twelve inches in trunk circumference (at chest height) and forty-four feet in height, the new state champion. Although pawpaws grow even larger in states farther east, nowhere else have I seen them dominate the understory. In two bends of Turkey Creek, we could barely see up through the pawpaw foliage, reminding me of some groves in the southern Appalachians where big-leaf magnolias fill the understory.

Green dragons with up to thirteen oddly assembled leaves grew to heights of three feet near Turkey Creek. Their pale green spears thrust outward eight inches from their pulpit-like spathes. We could hardly avoid stepping on green dragons, so numerous they were.

But an even greater thrill was the Indian pinks. They punctuated the foot-high green carpet of the floodplain at Turkey Creek. With vermillion base and five lemon-yellow petals, these flowers are a photographer's delight and challenge. They hide in the shade of big oaks and gums. A Stephen F. Austin State University team, in an ecological study of Upland Island Wilderness, only thirty miles to the southwest of Turkey Hill, never found a specimen.

Our greatest treat in Turkey Hill was the short-stemmed iris. From picnickers to botanists, most of the plant lovers

of East Texas have never seen a wild iris in bloom. Yet there
they were, in full glory, in the shallow abandoned channels
of Turkey Creek, apparently our only Texas wilderness that
has any.

Another joy of these bottoms was the spider lily. Although it had already bloomed in ostentatious white in
April, it had retained its two-foot-long fleshy leaves. We also
saw the two-tiered leaf rosettes of Carolina lilies, which
bloom there in September.

We saw few shagbark hickories until we closely ap-
proached the place where Turkey Creek flows southward
across the northern boundary of the wilderness. Then we
came across one after another, probably the closest concentration of mature shagbarks left in Texas.

With such a wealth of plants, Turkey Creek obviously
provides a rich habitat for animals. I had never seen so
many deer tracks. Squirrels and squirrel nests abounded.
The ground was almost porous with holes of different animal species. Barred owls were so tame as to fly and sit in
plain view at noontime. Broadbanded water snakes and cottonmouth moccasins were fat and sassy, refusing to flee until we banged sticks in front of them. Turtles slid into the
creek, lizards and blue-tailed skinks scurried ahead of us.
We saw many strangely painted insects. On this day we at-
tracted no mosquitoes. Our previous long day walking in
the warm woods without a bath intervening had armed us
with a protective odor.

By this time, although we were less than three miles from
camp, we had zig-zagged for about five miles. We stopped to
observe the many varieties of dragonflies and damselflies.
One pair, red and black, sat on a stalk in copulative embrace. I wondered what euphoria dragonflies experience.

We took a different route back to camp—due south, at
first, up the main ridge, climbing more than one hundred
feet in elevation through loblolly pine and white oak, and
then through shortleaf pine and southern red oak to longleaf pine and post oak. As we turned southeastward and followed the ridge, we passed under various combinations,
including stands of all three pine species. To look up at the
tall pine tops as we walked was like floating through different colors and densities of clouds.

Eye in the Canopy. *Where a big tree has recently fallen, small flowering plants are taking advantage of a few years of sunlight before oaks and hickories darken the opening. Among these flowers, the Indian pink stands out as a bright shaft of lemon yellow and vermillion in an ivy-green morass. Rare in Texas forests, this flower is usually so isolated from others of its kind that it would not be able to cross-pollinate vigorously, save that its brilliant colors attract from afar the species of insects that carry pollen from one blossom to another. This is a case where beauty is survival, and survival, beauty. That is one thing the Indian pink needs to know, John Keats notwithstanding. (Photo by James R. Jackson)*

Pawpaw Subcanopy. *You are now getting a glimpse of a scene that is rare for Texas—pawpaw trees 30 feet high under a hardwood canopy over 100 feet high. Here, along Turkey Creek, is the only place in this state where I have seen pawpaws anywhere near this size. You can see their leaves, almost a foot long, dangling near the top of the photograph. Few plants can survive beneath their dense shade. This grove includes one pawpaw 44 feet tall, rivaling the national co-champions in Kentucky, Michigan, and South Carolina.*

On the ridge, the understory was rich in farkleberries, plum-leaf viburnum, and eastern dogwood. The ground cover was comprised largely of elephant's-foot, Saint-Andrew's-cross, and wild indigo, all of which had finished blooming, and green-eyes and three species of sunflower in full bloom. Blue-gray gnatcatchers and white-eyed vireos provided the musical backdrop.

In this one-day walk, we had broadly sampled the eastern half of Turkey Hill Wilderness and were well pleased with what was there. A year later, Dr. Elray Nixon told me that his students had recently found nutmeg hickories along Turkey Creek just west of F.M. 705. Several of us have now seen them, from saplings to craggy veterans. This species is known only along a few streams in the South and is diminishing dangerously as we inundate the floodplains with new reservoirs, including the one under construction on the Sulphur River near Cooper, Texas.

In 1979, at the end of its RARE II process, the Forest Service had recommended the eastern half of Turkey Hill area for wilderness designation by Congress and since then had left it undisturbed, except for a few buffer cuts around pine beetle spots. However, the Forest Service had rejected the western half and had continued to manage it for pine alone. This meant that they had continued to burn this half to suppress hardwoods.

The next day, we walked the western half of Turkey Hill Wilderness. Southwest of the main ridge, Sandy Creek drained southeastward through a lovely valley, the southern edge of which was shaded by beech and eastern hop-hornbeam.

Farther west, along the western boundary of the wilderness, longleaf pine has become almost the only kind of tree. Here, by burning the undergrowth every five years, the Forest Service virtually eliminated the oaks, gums, and dogwoods, which ordinarily are scattered widely beneath an upland longleaf canopy. As a result, the population of squirrels, pileated woodpeckers, and other species that associate with hardwoods is low.

But after twenty years of protection as wilderness, other species will return, and the western half of Turkey Hill will begin to catch up with the eastern half in natural diversity.

Meanwhile, the western half provides a pleasant walking and camping haven for the less-discriminating recreationists. It also contains a thousand acres of potential longleaf pine/ scrub oak upland parkland, to serve as a benchmark for determining whether a stand that size can retain its longleaf component without prescribed burning.

Beneath the longleaf pines, a rich diversity of grasses covers the uplands. Tallest among them is pinewoods bluestem. Because of frequent prescribed burns, poison-oak and bull nettle have spread widely among the grasses; but this is a temporary condition.

Wilderness lovers and forest ecologists are watching intently to see what changes will occur in the longleaf uplands, now that the Forest Service can no longer burn the area. Experts agree that longleaf pine upland parklands depend upon fire to maintain their survival as a community. Lightning fires will burn our wildernesses. Will five hundred acres of longleaf uplands in Turkey Hill be a large enough expanse for lightning fires to spread to each parcel as often as they did before humans arrived here? When dogwoods, bluejack, blackjack, and post oaks return, will the lightning fires hold them to scattered occurrence under the longleafs, or will they eventually crowd out the longleafs?

Under a natural fire regime, will the grasses reduce the poison-oak and bull nettle? Will azaleas and pine snakes and other less-fire-dependent species increase? These are important questions for managers of longleaf pine forests throughout the South, as well as ecologists and naturalists.

The Texas Natural Heritage Program has classified longleaf pine/tallgrass series as a threatened community in Texas because of replacement by loblolly pine plantations and cow pastures. Dr. Bruce Means, of the Coastal Plains Institute in Tallahassee, says the longleaf pine/grassland community is endangered wherever it occurs, throughout the South. Turkey Hill and Upland Island wildernesses contain the only large expanses of this fascinating life system that will be left to nature.

Even for people who are not interested in the ecological aspects, the longleaf parklands in Turkey Hill provide green vistas for hundreds of yards through the pine trunks, a pleasant place to walk and to camp.

Geologically, Turkey Hill Wilderness has the second-oldest surface stratum of the five. Turkey Creek has scoured into the Cook Mountain Formation, about fifty million years old. The differences in soil from that in other wildernesses may possibly explain why pawpaws grow so much higher near Turkey Creek than in any other forest we have seen in Texas.

All in all, Turkey Hill is an area where large numbers of people can enjoy bountiful visits for many millennia.

Access to Turkey Hill

From Big Slough, you can take Texas 103 eastward 25 miles around the north loop of Lufkin and on eastward 28 more miles to Texas 147; turn left.

Take Texas 147 southwest 7/10 mile to Forest Road (F.R.) 348; turn left and go 4/10 mile to the northern boundary of the wilderness; walk in.

Or continue on Texas 147 another mile to F.R. 300, turn left, go southeast along the western boundary for 2 miles, and then turn left, east on F.R. 307 along the southern boundary for another 2 miles until F.R. 307 turns right to the southeast. Along these last 4 miles, there are many places where you can park and walk in.

To reach the eastern boundary of Turkey Hill by car, take Texas 103 to its intersection with Farm Road (F.M.) 705, which is 30 miles east of Lufkin. Turn right and take F.M. 705 south 2½ miles, crossing Turkey Creek, to the Bannister Wildlife Management Area sign on the west side of F.M. 705. Just north of the sign, you can walk an abandoned jeep trail about a half mile northwest to Clear Branch.

Turkey Creek. *For thousands of years floods from this stream have carved and fertilized the bottomland where the beeches, oaks, hickories, pawpaws, and Indian pinks hide out from civilization. (Photo by James R. Jackson)*

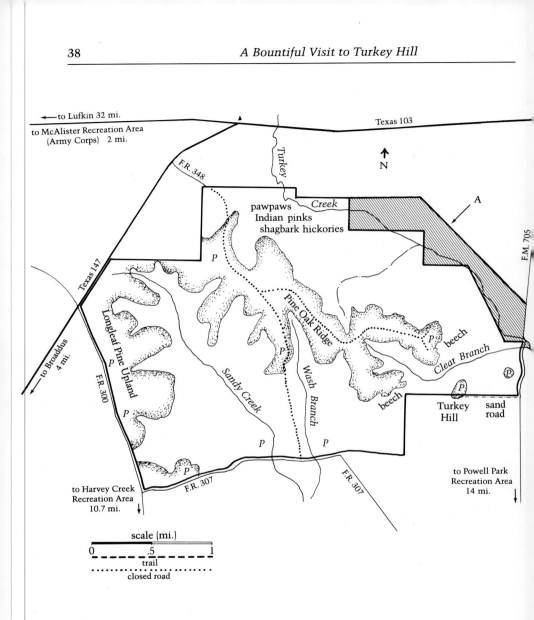

← to Lufkin 32 mi.

to McAlister Recreation Area
(Army Corps) 2 mi.

Texas 103

F.R. 348

Turkey

Creek

pawpaws
Indian pinks
shagbark hickories

A

N

F.M. 705

Texas 147

to Broaddus
4 mi.

Longleaf Pine Upland

F.R. 300

Pine Oak Ridge

Sandy Creek

Wash Branch

Clear Branch

beech

beech

P

Turkey
Hill

sand
road

to Harvey Creek
Recreation Area
10.7 mi.

F.R. 307

F.R. 307

to Powell Park
Recreation Area
14 mi.

scale (mi.)

0   .5   1

trail

closed road

Or continue to drive south on F.M. 705 to the first road
(sandy) west, which is about 6/10 mile south of the Turkey
Creek bridge. Turn right and take that road west about a
half mile to where it forks. From there, you can walk a hundred yards north to the top of Turkey Hill, where we
camped, and into the beechwoods and beyond.

Camping

Harvey Creek Recreation Area is a Forest Service campground about 10 miles south of the southern boundary of
Turkey Hill Wilderness. You can reach it from Texas 103 by
taking Texas 147 for 8 miles southwest to Broaddus, F.M. 83
east for 4 miles to F.M. 2390, and F.M. 2390 for 7 miles south
to the Sam Rayburn Reservoir. Harvey Creek has tent sites,
tables, restrooms, showers, and launching ramps. From
there, you can short-cut to the wilderness up F.M. 2390 and
F.R. 311 (1/5 mile east of F.M. 2390 on F.M. 83).

Turkey Hill, in the southeast, and any place along the
main ridge or west ridge of the wilderness, are good year-
round primitive sites to pitch a tent (P's on map). In the
winter, when snakes and mosquitoes are dormant, camping
is good along Turkey Creek and Clear Branch, on the north
and east, and Sandy Creek and Wash Branch, on the west
and south.

During hunting season (fall and early winter), the farther
from the roads you walk, the better your chance of privacy
and safety, especially if you fail to wear red or orange.

Trails

F.R. 348, 7/10 mile southwest of Texas 103 on Texas 147,
leads 6/10 mile to a roadblock at the northwest corner of
the wilderness. From there, it continues southeastwardly
through the wilderness. About 1 1/2 miles in, it forks, and
you can hike either fork. If you take the more easterly fork
for about a mile, it forks again. If you take the more north-
erly fork here, you can follow it another mile before it fades
into the bottomlands north of Clear Branch.

Beech Grove in January. To a growing wave of woods wanderers, winter is the prime season in East Texas, not only for its moderate climate but also for the enhanced vistas through the naked hardwoods, like this view across Turkey Creek. The old beeches lose their leaves in autumn. The saplings retain a distinctive leafy shroud. This grove produces thousands of beechnuts every summer and dozens of rich green crane-fly orchid leaves every winter.

White Oak near Hurricane Bayou.
*More than 11 feet around and 115
feet tall, this stately giant has
withstood the onslaughts of nature and humans for hundreds of
years. At its base, its buttresses
fan out to hold firm against strong
winds. (Photo by James R. Jackson)*

The Treasures of Indian Mounds

Picture an 11,946-acre maze of low ridges and shallow draws, covered with trees towering above a vast variety of flowering plants, some of which are seldom seen elsewhere. Zoom in on the trees and note that, on the slopes and in the draws, stately American beech and southern magnolia dominate. This plant association is vanishing from the earth, under an onslaught of indiscriminate clearcutting and pine planting. The Texas Natural Heritage Program in the General Land Office has classified beech/magnolia as a threatened plant community in Texas.

The higher lands of our maze contain the largest remaining stronghold of mature black hickory, a Texas species that laps over into western Louisiana and southern Arkansas.

We call this area Indian Mounds. Just outside its southeastern corner rises an assemblage of four shapely mounds up to forty feet tall, which local people and the Forest Service call "Indian Mounds." Nobody has excavated these mounds, although they superficially resemble the heaps of dirt that archaeologists have attributed to indigenous tribes from Texas to Alabama.

Indian Mounds Wilderness rises from the west shore of Toledo Bend Reservoir in Sabine National Forest. Atop one of its ridges, old American beech and white ash trees are the dominants. Dr. Elray Nixon, the leading plant ecologist of East Texas, has never seen such an upland beech/ash community anywhere else. On one of the old beeches is an ancient carving of a human figure floating diagonally while aiming an arrow down on a bison.

Four champion trees grow in this wilderness. One, a little-hip hawthorn, is national co-champion. State cham-

Beech/Magnolia Community.
The light-barked trunks are those of American beeches. The large leaves on the left margin belong to a southern magnolia. Modern forestry practices are eliminating this plant association, which once dominated the slopes above rivers and creeks from South Carolina to Texas but now is classified as threatened.

Liverworts Draped above Hurricane Bayou. *Here, spring water drips constantly from unusually large liverworts, one of the most ancient families of plants, instrumental in the breaking of rock into soil. The largest leaves have fallen from cross vines high above.*

pions include a flatwoods plum, Florida sugar maple, and eastern hop-hornbeam. The area also contains the largest white oak and black cherry in the national forests in Texas, along with a great variety of other tree species.

Shortleaf pines and about a dozen longleafs inhabit the uplands. Loblollies live in the uplands and lowlands. Possibly half the canopy trees are pines. Only on Beech/Ash Ridge are the pines almost completely suppressed.

Now that Indian Mounds is designated as a wilderness, the Forest Service is required to cease clearcutting, pine planting, and hardwood controlling. Eventually, all the stands will succeed into old growth. Pines will decrease to the minority hardwood/pine status they experienced before human beings began clearcutting in the nineteenth century.

The best time to see wild flowers in Indian Mounds is in March and April, when the ephemeral community of the forest floor effloresces. First bloom the violets of many species, including three white violets and a large concentration of Walter's violet, the leaf of which has deep-sunk, darkened veins. Spring cress and Carolina jessamine, with its yellow trumpetlike corollas, join the violets. Soon, the spotted-leaf trillium blossoms in great numbers.

Even when the southern twayblade attains its peak in March, the average woods walker would walk by without once seeing one, because this orchid is small and the color of its corolla blends with the dead oak leaves beneath it. It probably depends on oak leaves not only to provide the sand-buff background for its camouflage but also to deposit certain chemicals and to nourish certain fungi essential to its survival. True, it has two green leaves, but they are as tiny as turkeyberry leaves, unnoticeable to the average human.

The coralroot orchid hides even better because it never has green leaves at all. The reddish tan of its flower head evades the eye among the dried pine or red cedar needles that cover the sand. Every modern plant has its own ploy, its own partners with which it is interdependent.

Later in March, the green adder's mouth orchid unfurls its rich unicolored mouth and sticks out its spiky tongue. In April, three-leaved and rare five-leaved jack-in-the-pulpits bloom. The green rein orchis closely follows, and then comes the rarest of all, the yellow lady's slipper orchid, currently known in only four other locations in Texas and uncommon throughout its scattered range. Finally, in late April, the last of the ephemeral community to flower is the green dragon, with its long yellow-green spike.

In different parts of the South, the spring ephemeral communities include different plants. But across the entire South, there is a similar reason for ephemeral behavior. Since the component plants live in dark deciduous forests, they, except for the coralroot, must perform all their photosynthesis while the trees are bare and are not cutting off the sunlight. As soon as the trees don their heavy foliage the ephemeral community fades out of sight. Its species do not squander this short season of sunlight by pouring much energy into leaves and flowers. The plants are frugal. They store most of their energy in large roots or bulbs, to give themselves a good start in their next short heyday.

We see more crane-fly orchids in Indian Mounds than anywhere else. I think that is because Indian Mounds has a plurality of the remaining beech trees in Texas. I have never seen crane-fly orchids far from where beeches grow or used to grow. Crane-fly orchids require the same habitat or depend, in some way, upon a chemical produced by beech trees. This orchid has the most eccentric life cycle of all. Its single leaf soaks up the sun all winter, changes gradually to plum satin underneath, and then withers in March. The leafless spike bearing crane-fly-like blossoms shoots up in August. Its petals promptly fall, leaving only tiny pods containing millions of gold-dust seeds.

Wild comfrey and hound's-tongue are others of the spring wild flower species that are rare in Texas but grow in Indian Mounds. Even more rare are wood vetch (third record in Texas), everlasting, rabbiteye blueberry, and a rare pea, *Lathyrus venosus* var. *intonsus*.

In summertime, a beautiful but uncommon species is the Carolina lily.

In the fall come the squarish liatris, cardinal lobelia, and other showy flowers. And only in Indian Mounds, of all our wilderness areas, do we find golden Alexanders, generally a plant of Arkansas, Missouri, and eastward.

The area is rich in ferns, mosses, liverworts, and fungi. This is the only place in the national forests in Texas where

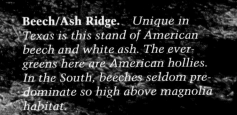

Beech/Ash Ridge. *Unique in Texas is this stand of American beech and white ash. The evergreens here are American hollies. In the South, beeches seldom predominate so high above magnolia habitat.*

we have found broad beech fern, rattlesnake fern, the rare wedgegrass, and *Scleria oligantha*, an uncommon nut rush for Texas.

Why is Indian Mounds so different in plant life from other wildernesses? Part of the answer appears on the precipitation chart. This area is at least one isobar wetter than any other Texas wilderness. Another answer is in the soil. Here, alone, the Yegua formation comprises the principal outcropping, including two major faults. In addition, Indian Mounds is drained by three particularly dazzling streams, Bull Creek, Indian Creek, and Hurricane Bayou—clear, clean, and cliffy.

Some of the topographic features here are different from other places. Above Bull Creek are exposed boulders where cliff-brake ferns grow. Along Bull Creek are soapstone banks, with symmetrical wavelines, and examples of an unusual community—beech/black gum/sweet bay, near some chinkapins. The chestnut blight generally kills chinkapins by the time they are forty feet tall.

Along Hurricane Bayou rise Fern Wall and Spring Bluff, thirty-foot cliffs cloaked with southern shield ferns and huge liverworts, through which spring water drips constantly.

On a smaller creek hides the Jug Hole, a rock grotto carved in a 180-degree alcove around a deep, cool, permanent pool, where pioneers once stopped their wagons to water their horses. Below this pool, the stream has cut through an ancient fossil bed where palms, tree ferns, and marine animals of forty million years ago lie exposed. This may be the only such pool in the region that humans have not impaired.

On the little trail that we have flagged to the Jug Hole, you come to a swale where sizable southern red oaks, water oaks, and bottomland post oaks grow with black gums, sweet gums, and green ash trees. Under this canopy, the carpet is covered with turkeyberry and, as the seasons roll, spotted-leaf trillium, jack-in-the-pulpit, and mayapple.

At the Jug Hole, a mile from Toledo Bend Reservoir, we once flushed a river otter. Indian Mounds Wilderness abounds in Virginia white-tailed deer, gray fox, raccoon, opossum, gray squirrel, fox squirrel, coyote, mink, weasel, and smaller animals. With the help of Ernest McDaniel, of Hemphill, we have here observed 186 species—almost every bird known to this region from anhingas and ospreys to 24 kinds of warblers.

Fortunately, the clearcuts at Indian Mounds total less than one thousand acres, less than one-eleventh of the wilderness. The best way to handle existing clearcuts in a wilderness area is to let them return to natural diversity. Prescribed burning is now restricted, so that other species beside pine may grow back. It will take approximately ten to fifty years for the managed stands to resume their natural appearance. Meanwhile, visitors can use the uncut main body of Indian Mounds, with no problem.

Three roads (one paved) are corridors excluded from the wilderness, providing unusual access by motor vehicle to the boundaries of the central and eastern sections.

A gas pipeline right-of-way bisects the Indian Mounds area from the northeast corner to the southwest corner. This grass-covered anomaly permits excess sunlight to enter the forest on both sides to a width of about one hundred feet, thereby inhibiting a few shade-loving plant species. Beyond that distance it has no effect. The pipeline is permitted to continue in operation as a corridor carved out of the wilderness.

Because of these corridors, the wilderness is divided into five sections, but these sections combine into one large forest, which human beings can traverse but no longer disturb.

From 1980 to 1984, an oil operator obtained permits from the Forest Service and drilled several wells in the heart of the area, two or three of which are still producing in 1986. The others were dry holes or produced oil and gas only for a short time, after which the operator pulled his pipes and moved out, leaving hard-packed drilling pads to resist the inexorable return of nature.

These blemishes are either small or temporary. In spite of them, Indian Mounds is essentially wild. Here live some species of herbs scarcely known elsewhere in Texas. Here survives the largest remaining ephemeral plant community west of the Mississippi. Above all, here remains the largest expanse of American beech/southern magnolia in the world.

Lady's Slipper Hideaway. *Southern red oaks and shortleaf pines shade this draw, along an upland branch of Hurricane Bayou. Here, in April, one of the six Texas clumps of yellow lady's slipper orchids blooms. This showy orchid grows in isolated populations from New Hampshire to Colorado but prefers its own eclectic habitat in each place and spends seven to ten years in storing up enough energy to bloom. The species is vanishing everywhere. In Texas, it is listed as threatened.*

Green Adder's Mouth on Upper Bull Creek. *Under fringe trees and Allegheny chinkapins, a green adder's mouth orchid shines. In Texas, this all-green species is known only to three wildernesses and a few other places.*

Access to Indian Mounds

You reach the wilderness by following Farm Road (F.M.)
83 east from Hemphill for 6 miles. Hemphill is about 30
miles east of the Turkey Hill turn-off, following Texas 103
and Texas 87. If you continue east on F.M. 83 for 2 miles you
come to sandy Forest Road (F.R.) 115, which runs southward for 5 miles as a corridor through the wilderness. If you
pass F.R. 115 and continue eastward 2 miles, you reach F.M.
3382, which heads south as a corridor through the wilderness. From F.M. 3382, at a point about 1.9 miles south of
F.M. 83, a sandy county road goes eastward as a corridor
through the wilderness past the highest point in the national forests in Texas, Rock Hill, to the eastern boundary of
the wilderness on Toledo Bend Reservoir. Four miles south
from F.M. 83, F.M. 3382 crosses the southern boundary of
the wilderness and enters Indian Mounds Recreation Area.

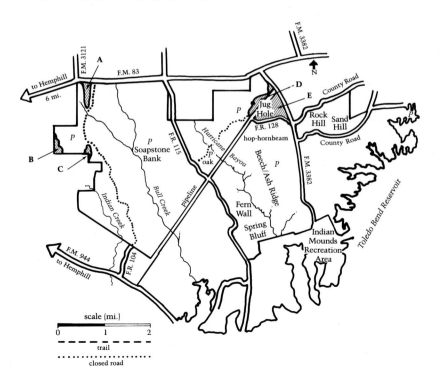

Camping

Indian Mounds Recreation Area, bordering on Toledo Bend Reservoir, contains 111 established units with well water and tent sites, along with restrooms, showers, and a boat ramp. Some of the best primitive camp potentials are along abandoned F.R. 128, running northeastward from F.R. 115 about 2 miles south of F.M. 83 (P's on map). Other good spots are east of the big pipeline and Hurricane Bayou, in the beech/magnolia draws. You can also camp on the shores of Toledo Bend Reservoir.

Walking

Until trails are established, the easiest walking will be along abandoned F.R. 104, which leads south for 5 miles from F.M. 83 about a half mile east of the northwest corner of the wilderness.

Bull Creek parallels F.R. 104, crossing under it about 0.8 mile south of F.M. 83. Along the west branch of this creek a great diversity of flowers and ferns flourishes.

Abandoned F.R. 128 provides a good walk between F.R. 115 and the big pipeline corridor. Everybody should walk down Hurricane Bayou at least a half mile to the great white oak. From where F.R. 128 crosses the pipeline, you can walk southeastward through some beautiful mixed forests. The state champion eastern hop-hornbeam stands here.

The Jug Hole (*overleaf*). *This deep, clear, perennial pool was the watering place of wagon trains of early pioneers. The rock lining is loaded with fossils. Fish are so numerous that otters hop a mile from Toledo Bend Reservoir to feed here. In summer, southern shield ferns bedeck the grotto wall.*

Upland Island and Longleaf Pine

As primordial seas rose and receded in Deep East Texas, the Neches River deposited delta after delta of deep sand, tilted downward toward what is now the Gulf of Mexico. Each time the seas receded, torrents churned through the earth layers. Occasionally, about one hundred miles from the Gulf Coast, the streams exposed deeper, harder deposits of whitish clay and stone, the Catahoula series, laid in Oligocene swamps and broad river bottoms, 37 to 25 million years ago, when palms and fern trees flourished here and ash in huge volumes blew in from active volcanoes in what is now New Mexico.

Along the knolls of deep sand that were later deposited over the Catahoula, longleaf pine attained dominance in upland parklands. From fossils, we know that the longleaf pine species has lived for millions of years. Longleafs in the Upland Island area go back thousands of years. Palynological samples have indicated that pines have been dominant on large portions of the southeastern coastal plain over the past five thousand years. In 1976, I talked to people who lived near Upland Island eighty years ago. They all said that longleaf pines a hundred feet tall dominated more ridges then than now, had much larger trunks, and were not as closely spaced.

Some of these observers remember only these giants, stationed in stately array across the rolling uplands. Others, especially the hunters, saw more than the big trees. Being interested in deer and squirrels, the hunters noticed a scattered understory of plants that provide a healthful diet for wildlife. These include species of oaks that seldom exceed fifty feet in height, often referred to as "scrub oaks." Under the pines the hunters saw scattered blackjack and bluejack (more descriptively called sandjack) oaks, farkleberries, eastern dogwoods, evergreen yaupon, and a ground cover of pinewoods bluestem and bracken fern. Many other species were there also, including the strictly local slender blazing star, the breath-taking purple-pleat-leaf iris, false dragonheads six feet tall, and certain mushrooms the mycelia of which are vital to the regeneration and growth of longleafs.

Varying considerably from west to east, longleaf/scrub oak upland parklands once stretched along a miles-wide line from Texas to Florida, except where, in ages past, the Mississippi and other mighty rivers cut huge gaps.

Around the turn of this century, loggers harvested these parklands. Unlike modern clearcutters, they permitted all the original species to re-establish themselves.

In recent decades, human beings have replaced many longleaf stands with roads, farms, and towns. The Forest Service and the timber industry have been prescribe-burning the remaining stands and reducing the longleafs to a near monoculture. When a stand reaches eighty years, the Forest Service clearcuts the longleafs and generally plants faster-growing pine species. But on the ridge in Upland Island, longleafs still dominate. Moreover, oaks, dogwoods, and farkleberries still survive, although in diminished numbers. In wilderness, they will regain their natural relative density.

Upland Island's western boundary is eighteen miles north of Woodville via U.S. 69, near the westernmost boundary of the range of longleaf pine. Its 12,700 acres make it the largest wilderness of the Gulf Coastal Plains west of Florida. Deep in its embrace, a person has a good chance of finding a spot far removed from other people, a pursuit that can be highly therapeutic.

In the south central portion, creeks have almost surrounded a 2,000-acre ridge of the Catahoula formation, the High Point of which is 250 feet above the bottomlands. From the Neches River northward to High Point and on down to Big Creek, Upland Island displays a wide gradation of vegetation associations within a three-mile transect (fig. 2). At High Point you can stand in the breeze and look out

Lone Tent in the Longleafs. *High on the ridge in Upland Island, campers enjoy free breezes, long vistas, and tent sites cushioned by foot-long pine straws. You will notice a shortage of other tree species, a result of overly frequent burning by the Forest Service until 1984. Now, under wilderness protection, each longleaf pine stand will burn from lightning fires only about once every decade or more, as before humans arrived here. Bluejack oaks, eastern dogwoods, and other species of moderate fire tolerance are beginning to fill their former scattered nooks in the subcanopy. In time, they will round out a natural life system of longleaf pines, scrub oaks, grasses, and a rich diversity of other species, including the breath-taking purple-pleat-leaf iris.*

Catahoula Rock Formation. *Near the top of the main ridge, long-recurrent rains have exposed a line of boulders with sparkling grains of mica, crystallized with quartzite, caked by ashes blown 35 million years ago from volcanoes a thousand miles west. This rock encases fossils of palms and primitive hardwood species. Alongside the rock stands a sweet gum tree. In the background, a dogwood blooms.*

across ten miles of forests. Two hundred yards from the top, ground water seeps out along an impermeable Catahoula layer, sustaining a lofty garden of rose pogonia orchids, ancient club mosses, and the carnivorous rush bladderworts and small butterworts. In this seep, a team of scientists discovered the toothpick grasshopper (*Achurum hilliardi*), one of six locations in the world where this species has been found.

Two miles east of High Point, Catahoula boulders six feet high protrude above a permanent spring, a significant geological site. North of there, Upland Island contains a sphagnum pond, where stands the national champion American snow-bell tree. At the next elevation downhill, southern red oaks and shortleaf pines hold sway. Farther downhill, along with the national champion barberry hawthorn, stand white oaks and loblolly pines, with hoary azaleas in the understory. Falls Creek originates in Upland Island, plunging past a pitcher plant seep, where ten-angle pipewort, yellow sunnybell, sugarcane plume grass, and several species of orchids grow, along with all four Texas genera of carnivorous plants.

High above Falls Creek on the southeast corner of the wilderness is an oak/hickory upland sandyland from which rains drain rapidly. Here grow some species of wild flowers found only in arid places.

In the Big Creek bottoms of Upland Island, American beech, white oak, and loblolly pine are dominant. Among them grow some big Florida basswood trees, including the largest individual of that subspecies ever reported. In this soil, and not elsewhere in the national forests in Texas, we found the bloodroot, purple meadow rue, and great Solomon's-seal, species that are rare this far southwest.

Graham Creek flows through an uncommon combination of cherrybark oak/southern magnolia/bald cypress before it passes under Forest Road (F.R.) 314 and enters willow oak/palmetto flats. Here, tall willow oaks, water oaks, overcup oaks, and shagbark hickories join in forming a dark canopy, and centuries-old swamp chestnut oaks reach circumferences up to 206 inches.

Here, on the bank of a small slough, towers one of the most magnificent trees I have ever seen, a cherrybark oak an

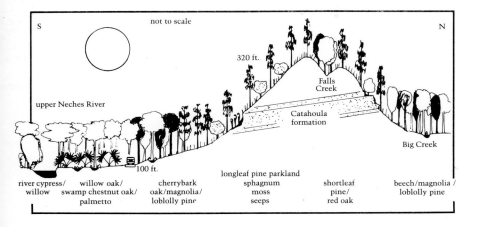

S N

not to scale

320 ft.

Falls
Creek

upper Neches River

Catahoula
formation

Big Creek

100 ft.

longleaf pine parkland

river cypress/   willow oak/   cherrybark   sphagnum   shortleaf   beech/magnolia /
willow   swamp chestnut oak/   oak/magnolia/   moss   pine/   loblolly pine
palmetto   loblolly pine   seeps   red oak

Figure 2. *This cross-section exhibits the diversity of the southern half of Upland Island wilderness. Complete local topographical transition from a major river (the Neches), through floodplain, slope, hilltop (the "Upland Island"), and creek bottom is contained within the boundaries. This variety in habitat permits several forest types and transition zones, the most notable being fire climax longleaf pine/pinewoods bluestem parkland, which is isolated on the hilltop. This plant community is listed as threatened in Texas. A public-access Forest Service road is excerpted from the wilderness as a corridor. The distance from left to right, south to north, in this cross-section is about 4½ miles. The rest of the wilderness extends another five miles northward.*

In the summer of 1980, a team from Stephen F. Austin University identified in this part of Upland Island 29 species of mammals; 91 species of birds; 36 species of amphibians and reptiles; 14 species of fish; hundreds of species of insects, including a bog grasshopper known to only a few other locations in the world; numerous species of fungi, including one collected only once before—in Florida in 1943; numerous ferns, mosses, lichens, and liverworts, and 456 species of flowering plants, of which 6 are orchids and 16 are rare, . . . and more are being discovered each year.

Rose Pogonia Orchid. *An April ornament of mossy seeps, the rose pogonia blossom begins a saga worthy of Scheherazade. The ovary produces a myriad of tiny seeds, which the wind carries like gold dust to other seeps. In order to be able to float for long distances, an orchid seed, unlike a bean or sunflower seed, contains insufficient nutrients to produce a leaf and carry on photosynthesis. Each terrestrial orchid depends upon landing near the underground filaments of a certain kind of fungus, which supplies it with enough nutrition to develop a leaf or, in some species, to blossom without ever needing a leaf. Since orchid seeds and fungus spores almost saturate their natural habitat, orchids manage to link up here and there with the right fungi. However, where human beings have caused widespread changes in the soil, it is difficult to transplant or to grow our wild orchids.*

High Seep. *Rains filter down into the deep sands of the parklands, reaching a layer of clay or rock and flowing almost horizontally along that layer until emerging along the hillside in trickles. At these outlets, called "seeps," sphagnum moss and primitive club mosses sop up the moisture and provide an ideal bed for many specialized species, including several orchids, visible in this photograph.*

astounding 165 feet tall, tallest of the state champions of all species of Texas. Its bark is rich and firm and marked only with the horizontal light gray bands that are reminiscent of cherry bark.

A half-mile to the east looms the state champion shagbark hickory, over ten feet in circumference, shedding big slabs of outer bark.

In the shady understory, the parsley haw (state champion), mayhaw (national champion runner-up), lizard's-tail, and sebastian-bush may compete with dense stands of Louisiana palmetto. These head-high palms, green in all seasons, stand in shallow water, as did the Oligocene vegetation that flourished here in ages past.

Fallen giants with root systems rotated upward house high, like the feet of a slain Goliath, evidence the maturity of this forest. Where the roots have been torn from the earth, water fills the holes. Snakes occupy these pools. This process begins whenever an old tree weakens to the stage where storm winds topple it, leaving an opening in the canopy. Hundreds of seedlings compete for the resultant sunlight. In a few centuries, one of them will take the place of the fallen monarch. I have observed such windfalls from British Columbia to Peru. They are a mark of an old-growth forest.

To traverse the willow oak swamp, a person usually must wade through two or three sloughs, up to knee-deep. But sometimes, as in the drier months of August and October, we have walked all the way through without getting our feet wet.

About a half-mile south from F.R. 314 and a half-mile west of Graham Creek, a gentle slope emerges from the swampy terrain. Here reigns the national champion longleaf pine, largest of its kind. Seeing this majestic tree is well worth all the slogging through dense palmettos. Differing from younger longleafs, its bark is no longer gray and ridged but is yellow-brown and in huge flat plates, like shining armor. As we stand admiring the champion, we speculate why the largest longleaf is down here beside a swamp, a mile away from the uplands where the longleafs dominate. Our most impelling theory is that, when the early loggers were cutting longleaf, they did not venture through these swamps to cut merely a single tree, no matter how huge.

Another half-mile south of this champion is the Neches River. Along the Neches, rows of river birch, swamp red maple, and arrow-wood viburnum line the banks, punctured on the eastern toe of the wilderness by sloughs with bald cypresses up to twenty-seven feet in circumference, the largest trees in the national forests in Texas.

Forming the southern border of Upland Island, the broad Neches provides a pleasant stretch for the canoeist and angler, including a three-foot waterfall extending from one bank to the other.

Upland Island also enjoys a wide variety of animal life. In the bottomlands, the rich populations of white-tailed deer and gray squirrels attract large numbers of hunters, in season. Graham Creek, itself, contains river otters and 25-pound broadbanded water snakes. Several colonies of the endangered red-cockaded woodpecker inhabit upland longleaf pine stands. The entire wilderness is good potential habitat for the eastern turkey, which already is re-established ten miles to the east.

The relatively large size of Upland Island provides an often overlooked benefit to wildlife—room for each species to maintain its own vigorous gene pool. The larger a habitat, the less likely is any species within it to weaken through inbreeding or for other complex reasons.

All five East Texas wildernesses have red-cockaded woodpeckers, but Upland Island gives them their best chance to maintain several colonies, which are far enough apart to keep distinctive genetic strengths yet are near enough to invigorate each other with an occasional Hiawatha-Minnehaha type intertribal mating. Parula warblers, brown-headed nuthatches, and toothpick grasshoppers are other examples of species that will probably benefit from the largeness of Upland Island.

Thirteen thousand acres may not be large enough to assure the survivability of some species. At least sixteen citizen groups are proposing that the Forest Service also preserve the longleaf/bluejack wilderness proposal (formerly called "Jordan Creek") ten miles east of Upland Island and the Longleaf Bridge in between, thereby forging a 36,000-acre chain of wildernesses. Although diminutive compared

Grass-pink Orchids. *After the rose pogonia fades, the grass-pink packs into a one-inch display as much beguilement as larger orchids of the tropics. A bee landing on the pubescent upper lip, which may look or smell like a bee of the opposite sex, weights it down until the bee's body touches the lower column of the orchid and picks up some pollen. The bee buzzes over to another grass-pink and goes through the same process. Some of the pollen from the previous flower sticks to the second plant, cross-fertilizing it so that it can produce seeds. No other insect has the right body for the grass-pink species.*

Pursuing the Same Prey. *This pitcher plant and squirrel tree frog are geared up to devour any insects that may drop by. Once a prey enters the opening atop the plant, the frog had better not pursue it inside or the plant may hold and assimilate the frog, as well. Nor does the frog provide a service for the pitcher plant. No symbiosis here.*

Foxy Frog. *Flower fanciers may assume that this green tree frog has a flair for aesthetics, but a cold-blooded herpetologist might contend that the amphibian is waiting to lap up the insects that fly to the fresh-blooming hoary azalea for nectar.*

to most wildernesses in the West, the resulting preserve would provide reasonable assurance that the endangered red-cockaded woodpecker would survive. Also, such a large wilderness combination would increase the chance that lightning fires would spread as far as necessary to maintain the natural health of the threatened longleaf pine/scrub oak/grassland community.

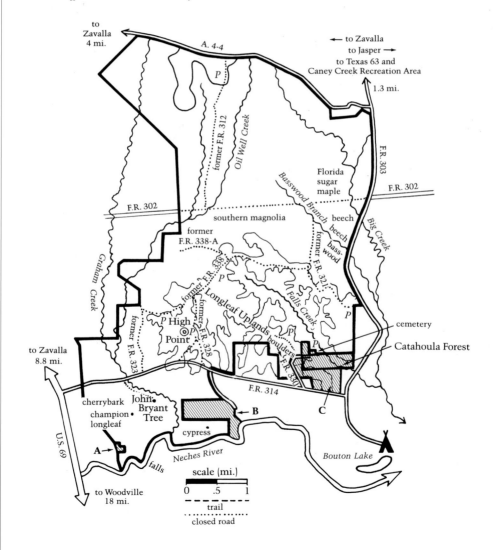

Almost any forester will tell you that hardwoods will crowd out longleaf pines if human beings prevent fires. Commercially oriented foresters stretch this observation. Confusing forest with prairie, they say that the Indians formerly set large fires, which raged across hundreds of thousands of acres of forest, incidentally controlling the hardwoods and thus maintaining the domination of longleaf pines. They say that unless humans set fires every five years the longleafs will eventually give way to hardwoods. They embrace this weakly documented theory as a justification for prescribe-burning longleaf (and other) pinelands. The Forest Service and many commercial foresters burn as often as it takes to prevent other species from growing up into the pines and sharing the water and nutrients. They favor pines because pines grow faster and, in addition, bring ten times the price of hardwoods.

Better informed authorities consider longleaf parklands as fire-climax communities, meaning that, in areas of sufficient size, lightning fires are adequate to prevent hardwoods from attaining dominance, especially the relatively small species that can grow in that deep sand. Otherwise, how did longleaf survive for thousands of years in the Upland Island area?

Closed-canopy forests with humid bottoms surround High Point and its longleafs. Very few fires could ever have crossed these bottoms. The fires through which the long-leafs achieved dominance resulted from lightning strikes within the highlands, estimated by an expert to burn each portion an average of every forty years. In wilderness status, prescribed burning for favoring certain species is prohibited. Lightning should continue to be sufficient to maintain the longleaf parkland. The groundcover of foot-long needles and cones would support ground fire without human interference, thereby keeping the trees spaced widely enough to prevent a harmful canopy blaze.

Upland Island Wilderness will provide a living example of what a longleaf/bluejack/dogwood parkland looks like after growing for decades without fires started by humans. It will regain its natural understory and once again attract numerous squirrels and deer, which now inhabit almost exclusively the lower elevations where there are more hardwoods

**Beech/Black Gum along Falls
Creek.** *Beside the clean water
and white sand of Falls Creek,
black gums often associate with
American beeches to provide
some cool, moist beauty spots
rich in animal life. Many black
gums are hollow, making good
bee trees.*

Anole in Rapture. *If you see
what looks like part of a vine
jumping rapidly through the
shrubbery, anywhere in the South,
do not be surprised if it is an
anole. Because this species
sometimes changes from green
to brown when it sits on a tree
trunk, the pioneers called it "cha-
meleon," although true chame-
leons are Old World lizards. As a
mating excitant, the anole can extend a cherry-red throat flap.*

and shrubs. Leaving it to nature is the only way anyone will ever know for sure what is the natural diversity of such an area. Forest managers are burning all other longleaf pine forests this size.

Unlike most wilderness areas, Upland Island has no mountains, lakes, trout streams, or deserts. But it has a rich diversity of ecosystems. By making it a wilderness, our generation is preserving one of the few remaining viable examples of our relatively gentle longleaf pine uplands. Because it is within four hours of the metropoli of Houston, Dallas–Fort Worth, and Beaumont–Port Arthur, large numbers of people can easily reach and observe its rich diversity. As wilderness, Upland Island will always be a significant part of our natural heritage, available for all to see and appreciate.

Access to Upland Island

Our largest wilderness is mostly bounded by all-weather roads on the north and east. The southern access is better yet—only one-half mile east of U.S. 69 on Forest Road (F.R.) 314, which meets U.S. 69 exactly 8.8 miles south of Zavalla, where a sign on the west side of U.S. 69 says "Bouton Lake." F.R. 314 passes between the Neches River bottomland hardwood forest and the uplands. An ideal place to park is near Graham Creek Bridge, 1 mile east of U.S. 69. Another 1.6 miles eastward, you can park by a cattleguard only a half-mile south of High Point. Farther east, another 1.5 miles, you can drive north on F.R. 330 to a good grassy parking area between an old cemetery and Catahoula Forest. Natural Area Preservation Association, Inc., owns this preserve, which is open to walkers and will be added to the wilderness in due course.

The main northern approach to the wilderness is from Texas 63. At a point about 8 miles east of Zavalla, where a sign says "Bouton Lake," you head south from Texas 63 on F.R. 303. In 1.3 miles a graded road (Angelina County Road [A] 4-4) joins from the west. A half-mile west, it becomes the northern boundary. Continuing south on F.R. 303 for another 1.5 miles along the east boundary, you reach F.R. 302, a good parking place to walk westward across the waist of the wilderness. Another 2.2 miles south, F.R. 303 leaves the wilderness, a good place to park and walk west through the uplands along abandoned F.R. 321.

Camping

The closest Forest Service campground is Bouton Lake, at the south end of F.R. 303, south of the east dead-end of F.R. 314, a total of 7 miles from Texas 63 or 6.4 miles from U.S. 69. Bouton Lake has only seven units (some without tables), water, and a privy, but overlooks a beautiful abandoned channel of the Neches River.

Caney Creek is a large Forest Service recreation area northeast of Upland Island. The main access is to take Texas 63 to a point 5 miles east of U.S. 69 and then take Farm Road (F.M.) 2743 northeast and east 4½ miles. Caney Creek has 128 camping units, each with table, tent pad, and grill. Near each unit are faucets, flush toilets, showers, and garbage cans. There is a camp store.

For primitive camping (P's on map), the longleaf uplands are superior—breezy, grassy, and well drained. The uplands along the northern boundary are also good.

Walking

What a variety! The easy walks are along abandoned F.R. 321, 323, 328, 330, 338, and 338A in the uplands and 302 and 312 through the body. From these, you can depart in any direction toward specialties like Falls Creek, in the uplands. Big Creek and Oil Well Creek, in the north, can be followed along worn paths and provide such features as large basswoods and Florida sugar maples. The national champion longleaf pine is a half-mile due south of a point 200 yards west of Graham Creek Bridge, an exciting slosh through sloughs sometimes knee-deep and palmettos sometimes chest high.

Swamp Chestnut Oak/Palmetto Floodplain. *This swamp chestnut oak, 17 feet in circumference at breast height, and its surrounding company of overcup, water, and willow oaks shade out most of the shorter species except hardy Louisiana palmettos, lizard's-tails, and a few surviving mayhaws. Graham Creek and the Neches River often flood this area, washing in rich nutrients for all the plants.*

National Champion Longleaf Pine. *Largest of its species in height (125 feet), trunk circumference (125 inches), and canopy girth, this tree has somehow escaped all the logging of the past century. Straight and sound, it looks every bit a champion. Almost everyone who has sloshed through a half-mile of palmetto swamps to the site has stood beneath this tree in awe.*

The Godmother. *Taller than any national champion tree east of Idaho, this cloud-sweeping cherrybark oak conjures up an eerie sense of mythical forests and ancient times. In first measuring the height, when I saw huge limbs at the top of this tree reaching higher into the sky than the acme line on my clinometer, I envisioned the great misty tropical oak that Rima climbed in* Green Mansions, *seeking to escape disaster. In June 1985, Texas Forest Service representatives, while confirming this tree as Texas state champion, remeasured it for almost an hour in disbelief—165 feet high, approaching the range of California's ancient redwoods. Even in Upland Island Wilderness, there are trees larger in circumference than this oak's 15 feet. But in height, the Godmother rules the eastern three-fourths of the nation. (Photo by James R. Jackson)*

Neches River Falls (*overleaf*).
The middle stretch of the Neches flows steadily and serenely into a sudden drop-off of two to three feet, catching many boaters unaware. They hang up or dump. The river is rich in largemouth bass and blue catfish. Clams the size of Whopperburgers feed on the rocky bottom. River birches and black willows shade the opposite low bank. On the wilderness side, from which the scene was filmed, oaks, gums, and pines stretch out over the river.

Forty miles below Upland Island Wilderness, a dam called Dam B impedes the flow of the river. After roaring through the sluice gates, the Neches resumes its gliding course through the Big Thicket Natural Preserve to the Gulf. Twenty citizen groups are requesting that the Neches River be protected permanently from Rockland Reservoir and other potential developments.

View from High Point. *Prince of the pines, because of superior wood and bearing, the longleaf once dominated the ridges of the Kisatchie escarpment from Woodville, Texas, to central Louisiana, in deep sands where shallower-rooted trees cannot compete. Beneath the well-spaced longleafs grew occasional bluejack oaks, prolific in acorns, and eastern dogwoods, which illuminate the spring with blossoms and embellish the autumn with red berries and tinted leaves. Today only a few thousand acres show a semblance of this plant association, now listed by some as endangered, by others as threatened. This view from High Point Ridge stretches from ridge to ridge for 5 miles. (Photo by James R. Jackson)*

Sunset in the Pines (*overleaf*). *As night approaches, wilderness assumes an even more primitive, thrilling aspect, carrying us back before the dawn of civilization. Sojourners become increasingly alert to sounds, like the echoing hooting of owls, ringing singing of tree frogs, and swooshing rustling of myriad pine needles in huge waves as soft breezes pass. Sing me to sleep, lullaby of the pines.*

By Log or by Vine?   *Life artery of the wilderness is this clear stream from which it derives its name. In narrow places you do not have to cross by log or by swinging vine. You can jump or even step across. During long dry spells the creek separates into a series of little lakes with water flowing underground between them. (Photo by James R. Jackson)*

Little Lake Creek,
the Roadless Place

Acre for acre and pond for pond, Little Lake Creek is as wild as any area in Texas. Only two paths penetrate its dense forest, the Lone Star Hiking Trail and its Red Loop.

The second smallest and geologically the youngest (Fleming formation) of our East Texas wilderness areas, this priceless emerald escaped for several years the prescribe-burning and other hardwood reduction practices of the Forest Service. In 1977, early in the RARE II process, that agency targeted the southern half of Little Lake Creek for wilderness, entitling it to protection from timber management. As a result, this portion had more hardwoods in some of its pine stands than any other pine sites of equal size in the national forests.

What a pleasure it was to primitive-camp anywhere in the well-drained uplands under the dense shade of medium-sized post oaks, blackjack oaks, sweet gums, and winged elms, along with the thin shade of the taller shortleaf and loblolly pines. And at the primitive campsite farthest south on the Red Loop, we enjoyed the increasingly rare privilege of gazing upward through the lacelike leafery of big, wild, black walnut trees. The Caddo used their hardwood for hoes, thereby perhaps contributing to the rareness of black walnuts.

This was a birder's paradise. The habitat was so favorable for a bird to hide at a moment's notice that even the great horned owls, barred owls, and red-shouldered hawks flaunted themselves before their binoculared viewers. Because of all the hardwoods, we could see seven species of

Along the Red Loop Trail. *A mixture of elms, hackberries, oaks, gums, and other trees thrives on the nutrients that floodwaters deposit here. In places, giant cane almost obscures the trail, an indication that no grazing is allowed here. This old American elm carries on its largest limb a load of ferns that unfurl in a minijungle after rains and curl up during dry periods—resurrection ferns. Every shade of brown pervades the deep shadows below, including obscure fungi.*

Texas Wax-mallow. *This relative of the Turk's cap brilliantly blares out that brown is not the only color in the shadows. We have not seen this species in the four wildernesses farther north.*

woodpecker and two subspecies of flicker in the same hour, a rare achievement in this modern world. On the west end of the wilderness, along Forest Road 244, there were six active hole trees of the endangered red-cockaded woodpecker within a fifty-yard transect.

In Little Lake Creek, we could see nature as it was before the chainsaw came. This area was one of the last to be harvested before the 1930s when the Forest Service bought the land for our four national forests in Texas. In most of the wilderness, the pines had not lived the seventy years required by Forest Service plans before becoming eligible to be clearcut. The northern third had two pine plantations totaling two hundred acres, planted in 1973 and 1977, and a recently thinned area. Left unburned, the wilderness would eventually grow back into an old-growth forest with hardwoods dominant in some stands and pines outnumbering the hardwoods in other stands.

Little Lake Creek was blessed in two more ways. Nobody had believed there was oil or gas here. Therefore, nobody had constructed high-class roads with Mars-like pads at the ends. And no cattle were here to eat the most succulent wild flowers and to trample the wettest ponds.

Enter the chainsaw and bulldozer. In 1984, as the East Texas Wilderness Act neared final passage, the Forest Service sold scores of acres of healthy pine trees in all quadrants of the wilderness, on the theory that the felling of these trees next to infestations would stop the spread of southern pine beetles. The buyers bulldozed roads, cut the pines around the beetle spots, and hauled them to market. As the pines were cut, they fell into and through the hardwoods and shrubbery, demolishing many of them. As mechanized skidders shoved and hauled the pine logs, they destroyed the ground cover, leaving a sandy wasteland. As multiton trucks hauled the logs from the "wilderness" en route to market, they mashed sand roads, which would remain for years. In one place, the loggers smashed into oblivion the largest fern bed, other than bracken, I had ever seen in a forest and wiped out a portion of the Red Loop Trail along the creek.

By mid-1985, at least twenty tracts, from two acres to about thirty acres each, were demolished and their soil compacted. One can only hope that these areas will return to nature in fifty years. Nevertheless, in what is left of the Little Lake Creek Wilderness, we can watch nature unravel to her pristine essence. It will be a sort of striptease of biological succession. In any one decade, you can enjoy the unmarred diversity and imagine what species will achieve dominance as the show proceeds, spontaneous and yet predestined by a gene pool that has been evolving for millions of years.

There are still sections where the day birds courageously sing and vie for dwindling territories. You can hear them amplifying at full lung from behind every leaf, into the dying light.

Already, like that of the day birds, the night chorus is in full climax. Not only the owls and chuck-will's-widows but also every species of frog and night insect ever known to this habitat offers its musical wares. Because of all the hardwoods and high retention of moisture in the sandy loam, tree frogs abound. And they chant and trill and warble from sunset to sunrise, even until, on foggy mornings, the sun is late to appear.

In addition to birds, frogs, and insects, the rest of the animal dukedom abounds here. Deer and other mammals are plentiful. Snakes and lizards thrive.

This 4,000-acre wilderness is built something like a bass violin, long and narrow at the top, bulging at the bottom. The pondy creek flows down its entire midline. The area rises gently on both sides to as high as ninety feet above the creek.

We have talked about the uplands. Now let's take a look at the bottomlands. Down by the creek grow the biggest trees—water oaks and American elms with resurrection ferns riding their large horizontal limbs as in a tropical cloud forest. Here also loom the white ash, sweet gum, bitternut hickory, and loblolly pine up to one hundred inches in circumference, and some winged elm, Carolina basswood, sugar hackberry, and river birch almost as big, all joining limbs at the top to nurture a dense, cool shade over the creek and its entire floodplain.

Those fortuitous sunbeams that find gaps in this formidable canopy encounter a second barrier when they hit the middle story of eastern hop-hornbeam, American hornbeam, red mulberry, and American holly. Shrubs include arrow-wood viburnum, plum-leaf viburnum, yaupon, and many species of hawthorn. Vines climb various trees to the can-opy—rattan, trumpet, and two kinds of grape.

With so little sunlight reaching the floor, it is surprising to see such a lush, green carpet—agrimony, green dragon, may-apple, Texas mallow, polygonum, boehmeria, and elephant's-foot. Fungi of all colors proliferate, including a tissue-thin white mushroom that melts in your hands.

Amazingly absent from these scenes are white oaks and swamp red maples, two staples of the other four East Texas wildernesses. Expected no-shows are American beeches. Their range ends farther east.

At one place the Red Loop passes between the usually shallow, placid creek and a small cut-off channel on its west side, where grow the remnants of the largest array of ferns I have ever seen in Texas. They are mostly Virginia chain ferns, with an occasional border of sensitive ferns, all about hip high, a bed of the softest greens. This side channel ulti-mately feeds into two ponds surrounded by buttonbushes and patrolled by green-backed herons.

With all of its fascinations, Little Lake Creek exemplifies the theme "You don't have to be big to be wild."

Access to Little Lake Creek

The wilder approach to Little Lake Creek is on the west. The key intersection is where Farm Road (F.M.) 149, at a point 12.4 miles north of Montgomery (or 15 miles west of Interstate [I.H.] 45 at New Waverly via F.M. 1375) intersects

An Opening. *Notice how the carpet has greened up where a big tree died and admitted sunlight. In this scene, polygonum is the adventitious plant that domi-nates the wet ground. In darker places, agrimony is the most com-petitive flower.*

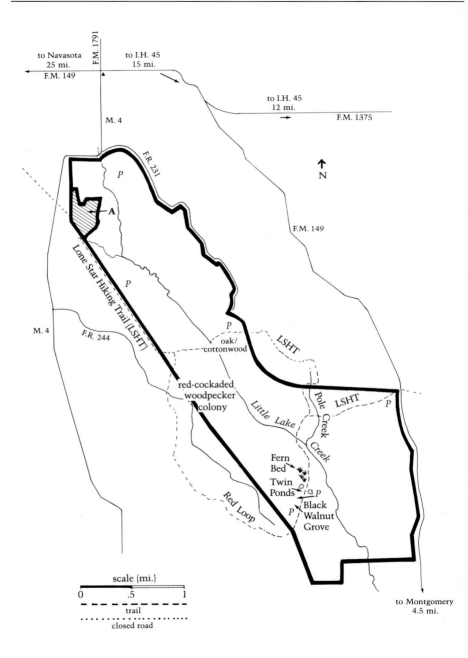

F.M. 1791. From there, you go south on asphalty F.M. 1791 and its sandy extension, Montgomery County Road (M) 4, for 4.3 miles to where Forest Road (F.R.) 244 enters from the east. Turn left and take F.R. 244 for 3.8 miles east and south to its gravel-topped end. Here you can park or car-camp. By walking down the two-rutted continuation of F.R. 244 for 200 yards, you come to the Red Loop of the Lone Star Hiking Trail. Take the loop eastward one step, and you have entered the wilderness.

Actually, after heading south from F.M. 149, you reach the wilderness boundary at 1.2 miles when the extension of F.M. 1791 takes a sharp right turn to the west. From then on, the road parallels the wilderness for almost a mile, until it crosses the Lone Star Hiking Trail, which exits through a gate on the east side of the road. You can park there and hike. Or you can go on to F.R. 244 and go down it 2 miles or 3.3 miles to fair pull-off places for car-camping.

For access on the east side of the wilderness, you can park, but not car-camp, along busy F.M. 149, 6.4 miles north of Montgomery.

Camping

Stubblefield Lake, a Forest Service campground with 33 sites, is on F.R. 215 about 2½ miles north of its intersection with F.M. 1375, 9 miles west of I.H. 45. It has water, rest rooms, and showers. Huntsville State Park, a large and lovely installation, is off I.H. 45, 7 miles south of U.S. 190. From I.H. 45, the park road leads west 2½ miles to the campground and lake.

For backpackers, there are many beautiful sites to camp, one of which is designated along the Red Loop. The latter is in Black Walnut Grove, 1 mile east of the dead end of F.R. 244.

Lone Star Hiking Trail

Take the Lone Star Hiking Trail westward from F.M. 149 (6.4 miles north of Montgomery). You will traverse some roller-coaster stream branches and ridges until you cross

Pole Creek and come to the junction of the Red Loop Trail. You can walk south on the Red Loop, for about a mile, crossing and following Little Lake Creek, itself. Under the closed-canopy hardwood forest along the creek flourish soft mats of agrimony, lady's thumb, lady fern, Texas mallow, and bottomland panicum. Resurrection fern loads the tree limbs. Vines of many kinds drape in junglelike profusion. In one stretch, giant cane almost blots out the trail.

Continuing along the Red Loop as it leaves the floodplain, you stir up a green-backed heron at Twin ponds; proceed uphill to Black Walnut Grove, a marvelous place to camp and listen to the rich night chorus. Another mile southwestward is the western boundary. If you proceed westward on the Red Loop, it will swing you northward for 2 miles, back to the wilderness and the Lone Star Hiking Trail, which you can take northward along the wilderness boundary to the exit gate on M 4, or eastward back to F.M. 149.

Fern Blanket. *It is pleasing to see a fluffy expanse of ferns in a wooded area. It is breath-taking when the fern-green blanket spreads through the trees for hundreds of yards, covering the entire surface as far as the eye can follow. On September 23, 1984, Little Lake Creek had the largest contiguous subcanopy fern field that I had seen on three continents. The species here are Virginia chain fern and sensitive fern, about waist high. On October 4, 1984, a timber company, after purchasing pines in a southern pine beetle sale, demolished all but a few struggling ferns, hours before Congress completed passage of the East Texas Wilderness Act. (Photo by Edward C. Fritz)*

Black Walnut Terrace. *In the up-*
lands, we can gaze at a vanishing
scene—black walnut trees in pro-
fusion. The Caddo Indians used
their hardwood for hoes; the early
settlers used it for furniture.
To the walnut's current misfor-
tune, it brings a high price today.
But it grows so slowly that the
Forest Service does not deem it
profitable to regenerate it after a
clearcut. Neither does any other
major timber producer. So black
walnut may be on the way out as
a forest species.

Beech Stand. Here, in the largest remaining grove of old-growth beech/magnolia in the world, American beeches comprise 54 percent of the trees. Beeches almost monopolize some views, such as this one. The bark on the closest tree is typical southern beech—smooth and pale, but flecked with lichens. The southern magnolia behind and to the left is more uniformly gray.

Beech Bottom, an Ancient Wood

East Texas hides another jewel, too small to be formally designated as a wilderness area because it would be over-trampled by visitors. Fantasize, now, walking in Beech Bottom.

You sense by the towering height of the canopy, the darkness beneath it, the owl hoots at midday, the hugeness of the fallen trunks decorated with mosses and fungi, the lush carpet of orchids in March, ferns in June, or big mushrooms in November, and some primordial ecstasy welling up within you that, here, you have returned to your source.

Your Being senses it. Your Being has experienced and recorded every stimulus of the environment on all of your human ancestors for millions of years. Your Being somehow tells you that you blend with this forest. Your Being likes it here.

But you need not depend on your feelings, alone, to recognize that Beech Bottom is that modern rarity, a forest never cut or impaired by human beings. With further pleasant observations, you come to know that Beech Bottom is truly the way it has been for many millennia.

You know it by the size and age of the beeches, up to eleven feet around and two hundred years old, as old as beeches stand in the South, where their hearts rot in the heat and moisture.

You know it by the grandeur of the southern magnolias, up to thirteen feet in girth and five hundred years in age, and the black hickories, including the national champion, and the oaks of many species—laurel, southern red, water, white, and willow—and two massive loblolly pines.

You know it by the height of the dominant giants—up to 135 feet. Even one of the American hollies here rises to more than 80 feet, the tallest ever recorded. Except for the magnolias and hollies, the great trunks are limbless for their lower forty feet.

You know it by the gradation in size from these scattered grandfathers down through hundreds of medium-sized members of the same species to the myriads of seedlings springing up in soft green beds. Three scientists from Stephen F. Austin State University measured this gradation in several species and found it to compare with the standards for an "old-growth" forest, one that is maintaining a dynamic stability undisturbed by human activity.

You know it by the diversity of vegetation—twenty-six species of trees, including the state's largest devil's walking-stick and sweetleaf trees, plus eleven species of shrubs and seven of vines, many as thick and tall as a tree.

You know it by the sponginess of the soil under your feet, a deep leaf litter into which you can dig your hands fifteen inches in one swoop and pull up a sweet-smelling humus, on which crane-fly orchid leaves stay green all winter and southern twayblade orchids bloom in March, before the beech leaves burst forth and obscure the sunlight.

You know it by comparing Beech Bottom with the scientific literature on beech/magnolia climax forests.

You know it from oral histories: Bill Hutchinson, now deceased, was born and raised within a mile of Beech Bottom. In 1978, at age 94, Bill told us the stand had not been cut during his lifetime and looked the same as always. His father told him when he was very young that it had never

Grove Edge. *Alongside the bay of a huge reservoir, the sun penetrates the beech grove in autumn, reflecting more browns than are visible in other seasons. Notice the lone loblolly pine in the background. There are only two mature pines in Beech Bottom's 100 acres.*

been cut. L. H. McCallon, who lives just south of Beech Bottom, and Earl Morris, who grew up nearby, say it is the best deer and squirrel area in the region. L. H. says he recently killed a canebrake rattlesnake here. Earl says otters play here.

So here we have a living relic of one of the major vegetation associations in the South, as it always was, an example for foresters and scientists to compare with what has become of our other forests.

Beech Bottom covers a hundred acres, the largest remaining old-growth American beech/southern magnolia stand. The Forest Service and scientists have alerted me to sixteen potential rival areas, scattered from Texas to Florida. Having seen fifteen and read of the other, I am satisfied that Beech Bottom is the largest and oldest.

We, the people, own Beech Bottom, as well as extensive lands to its west and north, all part of Sabine National Forest. Most of the stand north of Beech Bottom is separated from it by Mill Creek Cove, a blue, narrow bay almost completely surrounded by tall trees, on the western edge of Toledo Bend Reservoir. Motorboaters seldom attempt to navigate through the numerous big trees killed when the reservoir inundated Mill Creek.

Beech Bottom encompasses the middle peninsula of a series that jut a half-mile into Toledo Bend Reservoir on the eastern boundary of Texas. It is separated from Indian Mounds by hundreds of acres of Forest Service clearcuts.

Shadows of Ancient Times.   *In scenes reminiscent of old stands of European beech, occupied by Robin Hood, these well-spaced beeches still flourish. Elsewhere in the South, American beeches are being extirpated by foresters, who grow profitable pine trees in their places. In its 1985 draft management plan, the Forest Service proposes scenic area status for Beech Bottom, which would provide the beeches some protection from being harvested.*

Only to its north, across a cove, is some forest that the Forest Service has not yet sold for clearcutting—two hundred acres of it. Citizen groups, including the Texas Academy of Science, worked for five years to induce the Forest Service to designate all three hundred acres, plus an adjoining stand and the isolated cove of Mill Creek, as a research natural area. The Forest Service refused and clearcut the adjoining stand. The Forest Service proposes to build a trail into Beech Bottom and to classify it as merely a scenic area of only ninety acres, which they can change at any time and make it eligible for clearcutting. Scenic-area status would not be sufficiently protective of a plant community type that the Texas Natural Heritage Program officially lists as threatened.

We want everyone to experience Mill Creek Cove through these words and photographs but only a limited number of scientists and students to go there, lest we impair the naturalness that gives this gem its highest value.

People often ask, "How did southern forests really look, before the Europeans came? Are there still any stands that are virgin?" Since scientists shrink from the ambiguity of the latter term, we shall use "old-growth" to cover an undisturbed climax stand. The British, having no undisturbed areas, use the term "ancient wood" to denote an area that has not been harvested or plowed for three hundred years. Beech Bottom qualifies under all three terms.

In our five wildernesses, we can point to several examples that might be called "old-growth." In Upland Island Wilderness, we see no sign of timber harvesting around the giant swamp chestnut oak and longleaf pine, near Graham Creek. There, aging monsters are falling every year. Farther to the southeast, where dwells a bald cypress with a twenty-seven–foot trunk, men drilled a few shallow oil wells fifty

Gum Swale. *In a low place, the frequent rains replenish a shallow pond through most of the year. In this spot, the wetness-seeking black gum maintains a foothold against the surrounding beeches.*

years ago and loggers took some bald cypresses, but apparently nothing else. Today you can barely see any evidence of these early operations—a mostly buried concrete trough and a few rotting stumps of the rot-resistant cypress.

There is no evidence that anyone ever harvested the island between Big Slough and the Neches River, with its old swamp chestnut oaks and overcup oaks, nor the shagbark/overcup grove at the southeastern extremity of the wilderness.

Along Turkey Creek, as well, some of the big water oaks are dying of age, an indication that, if this strip has ever been timbered, the harvesters took only certain species, perhaps the white oaks, black cherries, and southern magnolias.

Those examples of old-growth in our wildernesses are all classified as southern floodplain forest, dominated by certain species of oaks, gums, and hickories. Although stands of that type have been succumbing to giant reservoirs, second-home subdivisions, pastures, and timber clearcuts, forty or more remain in the South.

But when we look to higher land for other types of old-growth woods, we find only one stand of any magnitude in East Texas that has never been logged. That stand is Beech Bottom, which, in spite of having been part of Mill Creek Cove, is above the old floodplain of the Sabine River. Beech Bottom fits most closely into the southern mixed forest description of A. W. Kuchler, whom the Forest Service employed to prepare its Potential Natural Vegetation map. Even more precisely, the stand is the beech/magnolia type the American Society of Foresters discontinued in 1980 because most of such stands had been eliminated.

In the middle of the day, you can sit on a log for hours and hear only the call of a red-shouldered hawk, the crash of an occasional limb, the resonant pounding and cackling of a pileated woodpecker, and, in summer, the incessant buzzing of forest beetles, the kinds that are dwindling in numbers as our old-growth forests are clearcut.

At night, you always hear owls, and, usually, the coyotes bark and howl. In spring, the chuck-will's-widows repeat and repeat, late in the evening, early in the morning, and whenever the moon is shining.

The dawn chorus features those species of birds that frequent big woods—Swainson's and worm-eating warblers, great crested flycatchers, yellow-throated vireos, punctuated by squawks from the resident heron rookery.

We should see to it that Beech Bottom, and a buffer around it, remain calm. The loudest sounds that humans make there should be the calls of scientists running transects, or the laughter of school groups enjoying field trips. These are the sounds of a research natural area. If and when the Forest Service designates Beech Bottom and a buffer on its north and west as a research natural area, Beech Bottom will always be calm.

Access to Beech Bottom

Beech Bottom is so precious genetically and ecologically that the Texas Academy of Science, the Texas Committee on Natural Resources, and fifteen other groups have requested the Forest Service to designate it as a research natural area, unavailable for recreational use. Besides, the only access, other than by boat, is through private property, a privilege the owner does not want to multiply.

Therefore, we recommend that our readers relish the area as well as they can by absorbing what we say and show in this book, thereby playing their part in permitting this magnificent area to remain pristine.

If you feel that you must see Beech Bottom, please do not try to get there. Write to Edward C. Fritz, 4144 Cochran Chapel Road, Dallas, Texas 75209. In due course, you will receive an invitation to a guided tour.

Crane-fly Orchids. *These are the winter leaves, colored plum satin on the underside. In spring, they wilt away. In August, flowering spikes spring up. Some thirty species of smaller plants and animals are interdependent with beech. The crane-fly orchid generally thrives only where beeches are or were, perhaps because of a common need in the soil.*

National Champion Black Hickory. *This tree, 135 feet tall, is the largest of its species. The range of the Carya texana is confined to East Texas and adjoining portions of Arkansas and Louisiana. Notice the tight bark with diamond-shaped ridges, characteristic of some species of hickory.*

Old Southern Magnolia.
This great evergreen exceeds 13 feet in circumference. Magnolias up to five hundred years of age constitute 11 percent of the trees in Beech Bottom. They are especially apparent, here, in winter, when all other trees shed their foliage except two big pines, some water oaks, and the tallest American hollies in Texas, up to 85 feet high. "Mother" magnolias, like this one, chemically inhibit young magnolias from crowding around them and reducing their underground supply of moisture and nutrients.

Index